W9-AHX-587

YAMATO COLONY

UNIVERSITY PRESS OF FLORIDA

Florida A&M University, Tallahassee
Florida Atlantic University, Boca Raton
Florida Gulf Coast University, Ft. Myers
Florida International University, Miami
Florida State University, Tallahassee
New College of Florida, Sarasota
University of Central Florida, Orlando
University of Florida, Gainesville
University of North Florida, Jacksonville
University of South Florida, Tampa
University of West Florida, Pensacola

George Morikami headed out to his fields on his tractor, 1975 (photo by Akira Suwa).

大和コロニー

YAMATO COLONY

The Pioneers Who Brought Japan to Florida

RYUSUKE KAWAI

Translated by John Gregersen and Reiko Nishioka

University Press of Florida
Gainesville · Tallahassee · Tampa · Boca Raton
Pensacola · Orlando · Miami · Jacksonville · Ft. Myers · Sarasota

Originally published by Junposha in 2015 as

大和コロニー　フロリダに「日本」を残した男たち

(Yamato Koronii: Furorida ni "Nihon" o Nokoshita Otokotachi [Yamato Colony: The Men Who Left "Japan" in Florida]) by Ryūsuke Kawai.

25 24 23 22 21 20   6 5 4 3 2 1

Library of Congress Control Number: 2019944091
ISBN 978-0-8130-6810-7

The University Press of Florida is the scholarly publishing agency for the State University System of Florida, comprising Florida A&M University, Florida Atlantic University, Florida Gulf Coast University, Florida International University, Florida State University, New College of Florida, University of Central Florida, University of Florida, University of North Florida, University of South Florida, and University of West Florida.

University Press of Florida
2046 NE Waldo Road
Suite 2100
Gainesville, FL 32609
http://upress.ufl.edu

To the adventurers who sought new lives in other lands

CONTENTS

PROLOGUE

Yamato Road

From the Canadian border to Miami on the Florida peninsula, Interstate 95 runs through the eastern United States for more than 1,800 miles. From north to south it passes through a number of states before finally crossing into the state of Florida. With few hills, the interstate traverses a nearly flat terrain in Florida for mile after mile along the coast of the Atlantic Ocean.

In 1986 I found myself driving south on I-95, headed to Miami from the central Florida town of Daytona Beach in an old Volkswagen Beetle without air-conditioning. After five hours on the road, and thinking that after another hour I would arrive at my destination, I began to take notice of the road signs coming into view one after another. On them appeared the names of towns coming up and the roads connecting them to the interstate. At one sign I stared, thinking, "Huh?"

"Yamato Rd," it read.

As a Japanese unaccustomed to reading English, I found it difficult to quickly recognize names on signs while driving by them on the interstate—after all, the signs were written with the letters of the Roman alphabet. But surely I had correctly read the name Yamato. Still, Yamato Road here? The name had appeared on a sign for a highway off-ramp. Was it coincidence, or was this really the classical name for the country of Japan itself, a name familiar to all Japanese? That was impossible, right? Maybe on the West Coast, but what chance was there that a connection with Japan would be found here in the Southeast?

At the time, I was doing a one-year internship at a local newspaper in Florida. Although I was an intern, I was one in name only and so did not have a regular schedule. While on the staff of the *Daytona Beach*

News-Journal, I used the two-story newspaper office, in the middle of a large parcel of land surrounded by palm trees, as my base. On some days I might visit retirement communities in this state known as a retirement paradise, while on others I might ride with the police and investigate crime scenes related to drug trafficking. There had been several places where I could have done my internship, even some in other states. But I chose Florida because I thought that, if I was going to live anywhere, it should be in a place that was unlikely to have a prior connection with Japan, a place that was novel and fresh for one such as myself.

When I made my drive to Miami, I had lived in Daytona Beach for several months. Since my purpose in coming to the United States was to see grassroots America, I probably would not have paid attention to anything that was Japanese no matter where I had been posted. But during my time in Daytona Beach there was no chance of that happening anyway. I admit I did meet a few Japanese living there, owners of Japanese restaurants and women who had married Americans, but that was all.

One day, out of the blue, a senior columnist at the Daytona paper told me, "A long time ago a Japanese lived in Daytona by the name of Oyama. He planned to race cars on the beach." Daytona Beach was known for its International Speedway, but because I had no interest in auto racing at the time, I took little notice of what he said. I didn't pursue the story of Oyama, and I soon forgot all about seeing the sign for Yamato Road as well.

When I was able to visit Florida again a number of years later, I had become aware that a park in southern Florida near Miami was named Morikami after a Japanese man. A museum of Japanese culture was said to be in the park. This Morikami was the original owner of the property; he had donated it for the creation of the park. What was especially surprising was that Morikami and a couple dozen other Japanese had come from Japan to this area early in the twentieth century to establish a colony that they called Yamato.

I was able to infer that the name Yamato Road derived from this Yamato, the early twentieth-century Japanese colony. But now I wanted to know more. Was it possible, in southern Florida where beach resorts had proliferated at every turn, to find out about a group of Japanese from Japan's Meiji Period? Who were they? What was their purpose in coming here? How did they happen to choose this area? What were their lives like? And finally, what became of them?

I had come to a place with no more likely a connection with Japan than anywhere else in the United States. Or so I thought: instead I found myself more and more intrigued by the lives of Japanese who had come here more than a hundred years ago. Having become interested in Japanese American history, I began piecing together the story of this Yamato Colony little by little.

Emerging from my research was the image of young Japanese with a dream, young Japanese who managed to rise to the surface in triumph after jumping feet first into an unstoppable wave of expansion and development that swept the nation and the state of Florida. While many settlers of the Yamato Colony were intelligent, educated, and well-to-do, in the end there was only one whose memory was to live on—a farmer whose name was George Sukeji Morikami.

YAMATO COLONY

Going to America
With a Broken Heart

**First Decade of the Twentieth Century: Amanohashidate,
on the Tango Peninsula, Japan**

For a distance of two and a half miles, pine trees form a canopy over what appears to be a bridge crossing the quiet waters of Miyazu Bay in Japan. This place of scenic beauty has been called Amanohashidate, or Bridge of Heaven, since ancient times, and it is mentioned in a famous poem composed by Koshikibu no Naishi (active early eleventh century):

大江山
いく野の道の
遠ければ
まだふみもみず
天橋立

Ōe-yama
Ikuno no michi no
Tōkereba

Mada fumi mo mizu
Amanohashidate

Distant is the road that goes
To Mt. Ōe and to Ikuno;
So I have not yet stepped upon,
Nor seen a letter from,
The Bridge of Heaven.

The Confucian scholar Ekiken Kaibara (1630–1714) visited Tango Province, where Amanohashidate was located, in 1689. He declared that the experience "was much like crossing a bridge over the sea" and that "naming Amanohashidate one of the three notable views of Japan [Nihon *sankei*] was appropriate."

Thrusting into the Japan Sea at the northern end of Kyōto Prefecture is the Tango Peninsula. From the southeast shore of the peninsula a sandbank extends across Miyazu Bay—this is Amanohashidate.

Amanohashidate exemplifies the ideal Japanese landscape with its white sand, green pines, and blue waters of the sea. Surrounding it are several good locations that offer commanding views of this marvelous sight, but among them one is known only to locals. It is Mt. Kanabiki, which rises to the southwest of the commercial center of the town of Miyazu. This mountain, which from ancient times has been regarded as a sacred peak, is 869 feet in height. On a ridge near its summit is a boulder that thrusts upward with a mantra of the Nichiren Sect of Buddhism engraved on its side. For this reason, the mountain is most commonly known as Daimoku-san (Mantra Mountain) by the people of Miyazu.

Shortly after the end of the Russo-Japanese War (1904–1905), a young couple was observed by the local residents strolling together along a path through the forest on the slopes of this Daimoku-san. He was named Sukeji Morikami; she was Hatsu Onizawa. Sukeji was the eldest son of a farming household in the neighborhood of Takiba, just downhill from the path through the forest. Born in 1886, he was eighteen or nineteen years of age. He had graduated from the local elementary school, afterward studying at an agricultural school and following

The scenic sandbank called Amanohashidate in Miyazu Bay, ca. 1925 (courtesy John Gregersen).

in the family business. Sukeji had a kindly face with downward slanting eyes, and although short in stature, he had a muscular physique.

Hatsu's home was located in the same neighborhood as Sukeji's, somewhat downhill from his. Five years younger than Sukeji, she was fourteen or fifteen years old. Tall and slender, she was a young woman with clear, unblemished features. If she indeed was fourteen years old, she was probably attending the Miyazu Girls Sewing School. When this school reorganized in 1906 with an expanded curriculum as the Yosa District Girls High School, it was the first such school for girls established locally. Hatsu matriculated there as a first-year student.

At the time, Takiba was part of Shirohigashi-mura, a village in Yosa District. The town of Miyazu, also in Yosa District, bordered the village. Miyazu was the castle town for the former Miyazu Domain under the feudal system. Through its business district the Ōte River flows from the south toward Miyazu Bay. About a mile and a half upriver, the Ōte is fed by a tributary, Hijiri Creek. Here, on the slopes above the Hijiri, Takiba is situated. Although the neighborhood shrine commands a fine view of the countryside, climbing farther up the slope soon puts one at Kanabiki no Taki, the picturesque waterfall after which the neighborhood is named. Surrounded by ancient pines and cedars, water cascades in several streams over the face of a rocky outcropping nearly 130 feet in height, sending spray billowing into the air. The coolness experienced here beside the pool beneath the cascade is delightful in summer, and the site is enjoyed as a place of relaxation and recreation that is well known in the area.

Taking the path to the right just before reaching the waterfall leads one past Mt. Kanabiki and soon to an open area. When Sukeji Morikami was much younger, this had been an excellent site for wrestling and other activities that he and the other children of the neighborhood enjoyed. From here the young couple apparently strolled deeper into the forest, delaying their return home until quite late. Hatsu's family became so worried at their tardiness that they considered calling in a *kitoshi* (a kind of shaman) to consult on the matter.

Although the two young people had been friends since childhood, in those days, young women had fewer freedoms than their male counterparts, and the eyes of the world could be a harsh judge of even minor deviations in behavior. Around the same time a boy at the middle school in Miyazu had been punished simply for accompanying a girl on a walk.

The episode probably gave Sukeji and Hatsu, who were mindful of what others might say, reason for concern. As a result, Sukeji asked for Hatsu's hand in marriage. He was well aware that there were others who had feelings for Hatsu and considered her quite attractive. Because of this he decided to act quickly and ask her to marry him before it was too late. Sadly, Hatsu's father, a master carpenter by trade, opposed the match on the basis of Sukeji's occupation as a farmer. In the end, Sukeji was turned down, his hopes shattered.

Seeking His Fortune in America

Not long afterward, a man living in the area approached the broken-hearted Sukeji and began talking to him about emigration abroad. The man said, "A friend of mine is raising pineapples in America," adding, "Maybe he could use you. You could come over." The man's friend had started a colonization project that was bringing colonists from Japan to

Florida in the United States. Sukeji was encouraged to try farming in Florida as a member of this colony.

While the Morikami family in its small farmhouse did not have the means to send Sukeji overseas, they determined that it might be possible for him to go if they secured a sponsorship for him. According to the 1906 publication *Saikin To-Bei Annai* (Most Recent Information on Emigration to the United States), third-class passage to the United States by steamship was ¥66, while cash required to disembark was ¥101, money for clothing ¥45, money for room and board in Yokohama ¥5, and miscellaneous expenses while on board the ship ¥6, totaling ¥223.

As an incentive for joining the colony effort in Florida, Morikami was informed, ¥300 was to be provided as a loan to cover the cost of passage and incidental travel expenses. In return, the new recruit was to work on behalf of the colony for a period of three years, at the end of which time the debt incurred by his passage would be paid off. A bonus of $500 would also be paid him. Since at this time $1 equaled approximately ¥2, in three years' time recruits like Morikami stood to earn as much as ¥1,000. In an age when elementary school teachers earned a monthly salary of ¥10 or ¥12 and a farming household enjoyed a monthly income of ¥3 to ¥4, merely seeing a sum of money like that equaling the promised $500 bonus was something to talk about.

Acting as Morikami's sponsor was a businessman named Mitsusaburo Oki, a financier of the colony project. Oki marketed raw silk and silk crepe in the town of Mineyama, on the Tango Peninsula. The silk crepe industry had been growing in the Tango area since the middle of the Edo Period (early eighteenth century), and by the Meiji Period (late nineteenth century) a number of companies had opened stores selling the local product called Tango *chirimen*. Mitsusaburo and his elder brother, Risaburo, established a wholesale silk business called Oki Shōten and opened a branch office in Muromachi, a mercantile center in Kyōto. Due to the company's success, the brothers had become wealthy men.

Dealing in raw silk, a leading export commodity, the Oki brothers were a driving force in the Tango *chirimen* industry who understood that market prices for silk were closely related to world economic trends. With growing interests abroad, they often traveled from

Mineyama, which had produced many talented businessmen like themselves, to countries in Asia in order to establish new markets for *chirimen* textiles.

A brother of Mitsusaburo Oki's wife was a young man named Kamosu Sakai. Kamosu was the third son of Takamasu Sakai, a former *samurai* retainer of the Miyazu Domain in the feudal period preceding the Meiji Restoration. An admirer of the inventor and entrepreneur Thomas Edison, Kamosu had pursued an education in business at New York University. He was the originator of the colonization project in Florida.

Struggling to make a living in farming while continuing to reside at home, Sukeji did not know a lot about the circumstances of the colony project. Moreover, he had never heard of Florida. He had an interest in geography, though, and after looking into the kind of place that the state was, he agreed to go there as one of the few actual farmers to respond to the colony's recruitment effort.

The economic situation in the Morikami household was dire. In 1892, when Sukeji was six years old, his grandfather had constructed a charming, solidly built one-story house and furnished it with well-crafted household articles that had been saved from previous residences. But at the same time, this grandfather had incurred considerable debt in paying the cost of construction and had lost the greater part of his fields in the process. Although he did not understand why, young Sukeji could not help but notice that the family's rice storehouse was always empty. He knew this because whenever he got into trouble—whenever he pilfered his father's best *sake*, for example, or tossed a friend into the river after quarreling—Sukeji himself would be sent to this rice storehouse as punishment.

From his earliest recollections, Sukeji's family had been tenant farmers with barely enough to eat. When harvests were poor Sukeji's father was unable to pay off his debts at the end of the year. While in his teens, Sukeji remembered his father having to write IOUs to those whom he owed money. As the eldest son Sukeji did his best to earn income "for the good of the family." But as his zeal became exhausted, he felt himself becoming estranged from his parents. As his relationship with them worsened, Sukeji became the target of harsh words from others in the neighborhood, who called him an ungrateful son. Under such circumstances, the $500 he was offered to join Sakai's colony was a substantial incentive indeed.

However, Sukeji's decision to go to Florida was not due merely to the attractive bonus offer. While cultivating the fields of Takiba, Sukeji longed to try something new as a farming enterprise. His idea was to acquire some land in the area, plant it as an orchard, and cultivate peaches and other fruit for export to Siberia, Manchuria, China, Korea, and other markets in East Asia. But he had to resign himself to the fact that, for the time being, his dream was impossible owing to the Russo-Japanese War.

Without giving up on one day planting fruit trees in Miyazu, Sukeji also dreamed of going to America. He would work a few years and earn the ¥1,000. Better yet, he would throw himself into farming in America, then return home once he had become a success. Surely Hatsu's father would then approve of his marriage to Hatsu. Before leaving for the United States, Sukeji made a solemn pledge to himself.

Japan's Emigration Fever

At the time Sukeji made his decision to go to the United States, emigration from Japan was at its peak. Between 1868, when Japan's government changed from a feudal system, and 1930, approximately 230,000 Japanese immigrated to Hawai'i, the initial destination of Japanese immigrants on a large scale. At the same time, another 107,000 Japanese immigrants entered the mainland United States. Of these, over 64,000 traveled to the United States in the years between 1900 and 1908, just before and immediately following the Russo-Japanese War.

When the signing of the US-Japan Treaty of Friendship in 1854 released them from the shackles of national isolation that prevailed during the feudal period, Japanese at last could travel overseas. To pursue educations, make better lives for themselves, or follow dreams of a quick fortune, emigrants bound first for Hawai'i, then the United States, Canada, Mexico, Brazil, Peru, Australia, and Southeast Asia poured out of Japan as though a dam had burst.

Some immigration to North America was by chance. Such instances include those of John Manjiro and Joseph Heco, two Japanese whom storms blew far from Japan's coastal waters in the 1840s and early 1850s.

Passing American ships found one shipwrecked on an island and the other adrift in the Pacific Ocean. Other early immigrants included Japanese employed as crew members aboard foreign ships, sometimes accompanied by women traveling for the purpose of prostitution, although not often of their own volition.

An early example of Japanese who made the determination to leave Japan of their own free will were the 153 immigrants who, in 1868, were the first to enter Hawai'i. They did so as farm laborers for the sugarcane fields, and they are known in Japanese emigration history as the *gannen-mono*, or the "First-Year People," because 1868 was the first year of the new Meiji government. Making arrangements for the group was Eugene Van Reed, the consul general in Japan representing the Kingdom of Hawai'i. When the Meiji government got wind of his activities, it refused to allow his recruits to depart, but they did so anyway.

Similarly, another group of immigrants sailed from Japan in 1869 without first receiving permission. The Boshin Civil War, in which supporters of the feudal regime fought the incoming Meiji government, had just ended. A group from the defeated Aizu Domain, fearing reprisals, decided to seek refuge in California. How they happened to make their way from Japan is not entirely clear, but what is known is that they followed a plan devised by John Henry Schnell, a Prussian of Dutch ancestry who held the post of military affairs advisor to the domain.

Taking with him twenty or so refugees, Schnell booked passage on a ship bound for San Francisco. From there his group headed inland to a location not far from where the California gold rush had begun twenty years earlier. Settling in the foothills of the Sierra Nevada Mountains east of the present-day state capital of Sacramento, the refugees established a farming enterprise that they called the Wakamatsu Tea and Silk Farm Colony. Within two years, however, soil deficiencies and lack of rain had taken their toll.

Telling the colonists that he was returning to Japan to raise money for the colony, Schnell left and was never heard from again. The Aizu settlers, who did not understand English, were left to their own devices, and they survived only by finding employment with the owners of nearby farms. One of the settlers, a young woman whose name was Okei, soon died of illness at the age of nineteen. Despite their destitute condition and scarce resources, the group erected a gravestone dedicated to her. It remains today at the site of the former colony near Coloma, California, a reminder for future generations of the colony's story.

Meanwhile in Hawai'i, laborers were needed from abroad to work on the sugar plantations. For this reason, the Hawai'ian government strongly encouraged the Japanese government to allow the recruitment of immigrants to work as farm laborers. Because of the impoverished conditions of farming villages in Japan and the necessity of reducing the population, the Japanese government agreed to Hawai'i's request, and the two countries signed an agreement that allowed close to 30,000 to leave Japan as *kanyaku imin*, or "government-sponsored immigrants," between 1885 and 1894.

After 1894, a number of private emigration companies appeared on the scene. They acted as middlemen between immigrants coming from Japan and potential overseas employers by assisting with the emigration process. Emigrants privately contracted by these emigration companies accepted advances on their future wages to pay for passage to Hawai'i. Called *keiyaku imin*, or "contract immigrants," they became the norm.

Because such a system could easily exploit the immigrant, it was forbidden in the United States. In Hawai'i, contract provisions did not always reflect actual conditions where contract Japanese laborers were assigned, and the problem of their mistreatment became evident. As a result, this practice of contract immigration was abolished, although agents for emigration companies and shipping companies continued to recruit emigrants.

Instead of contract immigration, immigration of private individuals through the emigration companies then became mainstream in Hawai'i. Like young bamboo shoots after a rain, emigration companies and organizations like them appeared in response to emigration fever in Japan. Bringing emigrant laborers to Hawai'i was neither more nor less profitable under the new system than it had been under the old, but the industry did attract a number of unscrupulous people who were engaged in unethical practices like taking larger commissions than those to which they were entitled. For this reason, Japan enacted the Emigration Protection Act in 1896 to regulate the industry.

Emigrant Japanese traveling individually to the United States depended on relatives and others from their hometowns to find work through fellow countrymen acting as intermediaries. In cases where the immigrant was employed as a laborer, a considerable variety of employment opportunities were available. In contrast, most work in Hawai'i was in the sugarcane fields. Japanese immigrant laborers were earning wages working on farms and in railroad construction sites, in seafood processing plants and lumber mills, in mines and other places. They were engaged in operating hotels and groceries and other retail businesses. In coastal urban centers such as San Francisco, many young men also attended school while working in domestic positions.

One impetus for emigration in Meiji Period Japan was the revision of the land tax, which made the lives of farming households more difficult. Another was the widely held belief that someone working in the United States could realize an income several times greater than was possible in Japan, and that even someone who was self-employed in Japan stood to earn considerably more in America. In addition, talk of the success achieved by others from the same district who had previously gone to America of course stirred the desire to follow in these individuals' footsteps.

Publications, too, vigorously fanned the emigration fever. Guidebooks that encouraged travel to the US and reported on conditions there, with titles such as *To-Bei Annai* (Guide to Traveling to America, 1901), *Beikoku Tokō Annai* (Guide to Sailing for America, 1902), *Kaigai Dekasegi Annai* (Guide to Working Away from Home Overseas, 1902), and *Shinsen To-Bei Annai* (Newly Compiled Guide to Traveling to America, 1906), were published in rapid succession, as were books that introduced practical ways of preparing Western cuisine and related subjects.

Organizations that encouraged emigration and offered support were established as well. Japanese socialist Sen Katayama (1859–1933) earned degrees from American universities and acquired work experience in the United States while also taking part in the establishment and management of a rice plantation in Texas. In 1902 he founded an organization called the To-Bei Kyōkai (American Immigration Association) and produced reports and articles promoting immigration. Similarly,

Christian minister Hyōdayū Shimanuki (1866–1913) contributed to enthusiasm for immigration to the US by forming an organization called the Nihon Rikkōkai (Japan Empowerment Association).

In his book *To-Bei no Hiketsu* (Secrets of Emigration to America), Sen Katayama wrote about the appeal of the United States as a destination for immigrants:

> Why do so many young people wish to go to America? Because it is to their benefit to do so. Often my fellow countrymen achieve their goals by going to America. If someone has the goal of obtaining an education, he can do it in America. If someone wishes to master a technical skill, likewise, he goes to America to learn it, only then returning to Japan. Person after person has the goal of making a fortune. They return home after achieving this goal in America. It seems that there is no limit to what one can do in America. Our experiences over a period of twenty to thirty years have proven it.

Katayama seems to be saying that, whatever goal emigrants may have in going to the US, be it in education, art, technology, or business, they can achieve it. Katayama himself came to the United States penniless. While holding down a job, he managed to earn a university degree, demonstrating by his own example the truth in what he wanted to convey.

Katayama's other examples of individuals who had had few resources but nevertheless were able to succeed in life included oil king John D. Rockefeller (1839–1937). To Katayama, the society that made a success such as his possible was indeed admirable. Again, witness his own words:

> The president of his own steel trust, [Charles M.] Schwab rose quickly to being a leading player in the steel industry after starting out as an apprentice in a laundry. The reader has certainly heard of Rockefeller. He began as a mere head clerk in a store. Also employed as a tailor, he became president [of his own company]. [Thomas] Edison was a person who finished [as a success] after first hawking newspapers to railroad passengers. Looking at it one

way, American society gives young people who start out living in poverty the opportunity to become successes in life.

In emigration magazines and other publications, advertising connected to travel to the US was displayed in a manner meant to attract attention. Beginning with men's apparel, magazine ads also endorsed everything from medicine to prevent seasickness ("Motion Sickness Medicine for On Board Ship!" read one such ad, "For All Who Are Going Abroad to America, an Effective Remedy That Is Indispensable!") to cooking schools that offered "classes in American-style cooking." (Ads might make use of the occasional English word to validate their message, as did the one just quoted, which substituted the English "cook" (*kukku*) for a Japanese-language equivalent.) An advertisement that stated, "Our business provides a measure of convenience for the gentleman who is starting out on his first voyage to America or Hawai'i" was for an inn located in the harbor district of Yokohama, one of the points of departure for traveling overseas to the United States.

Such advertising was aimed at students who would be supporting themselves in the US by working in addition to studying. The ads not only addressed questions such as the importance of going to America but also offered specific practical information on such matters as applying for a passport, booking passage overseas, obtaining work in the US, and learning the fundamentals of English conversation.

The reasons that emigrants had for going to the United States were not many, but they were varied. Often Japanese sought to leave their country in order to escape pressures in society. For some it was government oppression, for others conscription into the military. Many were appalled by the large numbers of casualties in the Sino-Japanese and Russo-Japanese Wars. Moreover, some immigrants fled discrimination and ostracism in their communities.

It is often said that in farming households family members other than the eldest son go overseas because they find making a living at home difficult. This is not necessarily so. Numerous examples exist of the eldest son, or rather the eldest son and the father, going to the United States to work temporarily, a practice known as *dekasegi*. In general, learning that the father and the older brother were successful inspired others back home to follow them.

Morikami too was an eldest son. In addition to his dream of one day planting orchards, he had a will and a passion to turn his life around and make a success of himself in order to return to his hometown in glory. By the time that he decided to go to America, emigration fever in Japan had increased, but so had anti-Japanese sentiment in the place where the Japanese immigrant population in the United States was greatest— on the West Coast. Although the Japanese government had imposed limitations on immigration to America, the anti-Japanese movement on the West Coast did not abate. The governments of the two countries then worked out a consensus on the issue in the form of the Gentlemen's Agreement of 1908, a secret exchange of diplomatic notes that had the effect of greatly curtailing the numbers of Japanese entering the US. Happily for him, Morikami had already applied for and been issued a passport to enter America two years earlier, in 1906.

Since 1885, when Japan had begun regulating emigration in accordance with an agreement between the Meiji government and the Kingdom of Hawai'i, the issuing of passports had rapidly increased with emigration. About the time that Morikami first began to consider going to the United States, a permit to travel abroad issued by a government office was necessary. To apply for a passport, at least two people were required as guarantors.

Morikami applied for his passport at the Kyōto Prefectural Office. Filling out his application, he identified himself as "Morikami Sukeji, commoner, head of household." He gave the name of his destination as "United States of America" (Hokubei Gasshūkoku), and he stated that his reason for travel was "To engage in farming." Listed as his guarantors were five prominent individuals from his neighborhood of Takiba, including Yasusauemon Kusuda and Kurazo Kurahashi.

After acquiring his passport in the spring of 1906, Morikami was set to depart. But before leaving Miyazu, he saw Hatsu one last time. He met her on the crowded main street of Miyazu, the town's center since the days of the old feudal domain. Knowing that he was bound for America, Sukeji bid Hatsu farewell.

Setting Sail—An Ocean and a Continent to Cross

Sukeji's father was named Takezō, his mother Soyo. Beginning with Sukeji, the couple had six children, four boys and two girls. Whether their oldest son received their blessing for his trip to America is unknown.

When Sukeji left home at age nineteen, his youngest brother, Yoneji, was not yet five years old. Sukeji often played with Yoneji around a stone lantern that was near their house. Sometimes Yoneji would give Sukeji a fright by attempting to climb a flight of stone steps near the lantern without falling. The two were quite close, but Yoneji probably understood only that his older brother was going somewhere far away. On the morning of Morikami's departure, Yoneji ran after him, weeping. "Don't cry," Sukeji told Yoneji, "Before long Nii [Elder Brother—that is, Sukeji himself] will come back." For a long time Yoneji's tearstained face remained pressed against Sukeji's chest.

In 1906 a regular shipping route connected Hong Kong with the West Coast of the United States. A ship departing from Hong Kong sailed by way of Shanghai to call at the Japanese ports of Moji, in northern Kyūshū, as well as Kōbe and Yokohama, then sailed across the Pacific Ocean to either Seattle or San Francisco. Morikami had planned to board a ship in Kōbe bound for Seattle but was detained in Kyōto in order to undergo treatment for his eyes. The reason for his detention was that passengers with infectious diseases such as trachoma would not be allowed to disembark upon arrival in the United States.

In nearly all cases of emigration from Japan, the formalities of traveling to the US like arrangements for lodging prior to departure were left to the many private emigration companies. Because the number of people who had booked passage overseas was so great, it was usual for them before sailing to stay in one of the large number of lodging houses in Kōbe or Yokohama. Travelers could not say how many days they would have to wait to board a ship.

In March 1906, Morikami spent as long as a month in Kyōto, taking walks around the city to see a few of the sights between eye treatments. The time spent in Kyōto was not only his first opportunity to see Japan, it was also his last. With the condition of his eyes improving, Morikami went to Arashiyama, a suburb of Kyōto, to view the cherry blossoms but found that they had already fallen, and that new green leaves had taken their place. At the river nearby, women were filling tubs with water and washing vegetables. Kyōto vegetables, which Morikami saw were of especially fine quality, were also quite expensive. Still, no matter how fine or expensive they were, he felt that they could not taste as good as the vegetables his own mother prepared at home.

While his feet carried him to every corner of the city, Morikami found that the sights of Kyōto were not as magnificent as he had expected them to be. For the most part he just passed them by without stopping, as he did not have any extra cash in his pockets. One place Morikami went to several times was a shop on the outskirts of the city selling roasted sweet potatoes, where he would buy a large bagful for as little as two or three *sen*. Other than that, he spent much of the remainder of his time at a used bookstore near his lodgings.

From the time he was a child Sukeji liked to read books. During the lengthening evenings of autumn, while feeding the fire in the open hearth with pine logs, warming himself, and carrying the infant Yoneji around on his back, Sukeji would become engrossed in reading adventure novels by the firelight. He got into the habit of reading this way because his parents worked late into the evening by the light of the only kerosene lamp that the family owned.

The woman who ran the used bookstore did not view Morikami with disapproval even though he spent his time there reading the books without buying any. When at last the time came for him to leave Kyōto, he purchased several books at the bookstore, including a large volume on Japanese history and an adventure novel he particularly liked, *Ukishiro Monogatari* (The Story of Battleship *Ukishiro*, 1890). Written by Ryūkei Yano (1851–1931), the novel was a new kind of adventure story for an age in which the eyes of a nation were opening to possibilities overseas. Reflecting a romanticized version of Morikami's own dreams, the book is about a Japanese youth who sets out to visit foreign lands, just as Morikami himself was doing. Encountering pirates, the youth steals their ship, named the *Ukishiro* (*Floating Castle*), and sails off to join forces with the people of Indonesia and Java who are fighting for independence. Later in the novel, the youth joins the crew of a Japanese naval academy training vessel that is shipwrecked on a remote island near the Strait of Magellan, where the naval cadets fall in love with the island maidens. This kind of plot made Morikami's heart beat faster.

Morikami paid his money to the woman in the bookstore, whose face had become so familiar to him. As he gathered up his purchases, he announced, "From here I'm going to America. I'll read these on the ship." Perhaps responding to a sense of loneliness that she saw in him, she said, "*Maa*" (oh), as a tear ran down her cheek.

The ship on which Morikami sailed was a passenger steamer called the *Shinano-Maru* (total tonnage: 6,388 tons), which had plied a regular route between Hong Kong, Japan, and Seattle for the Nippon Yūsen Kaisha shipping company since beginning service in 1896. In 1903, three years before Sukeji made his voyage, the celebrated author Kafū Nagai (1879–1959) had also sailed aboard this vessel to Seattle. When the Russo-Japanese War began, it was requisitioned by the military as an auxiliary cruiser and later gained fame for its role in an important sea battle.

In fact, during the war the *Shinano-Maru* sighted the Russian Baltic Fleet while on patrol in the Strait of Tsushima and quickly alerted the combined fleet of the Japanese Imperial Navy to its discovery. On the basis of the *Shinano-Maru's* report, the combined fleet wired a communiqué to Imperial Command that is well known to history. "Have received warning that the enemy fleet has been sighted," the message read. "The combined fleet was immediately dispatched to engage and destroy the enemy. Today's weather fair with high waves." Morikami, who liked history, probably knew all of this information about the ship that was taking him to America. He must have thought this a propitious start to his adventure.

During a cold rain on the morning of April 8, 1906, the *Shinano-Maru*, sailing with passenger Sukeji Morikami and others, left the port of Yokohama behind. In a little while, when the steamer neared the Izu Peninsula and Ōshima Island, Morikami watched as Mt. Fuji, magnificent with clouds towering above it, suddenly came into view. At that moment, a line of poetry came to mind:

白扇倒懸東海天

Hakusen sakashima ni kakaru tōkai no ten

A white fan hangs inverted in the heavens above the eastern sea.

It was a line from a quatrain (*shichigon-zekku*) titled "Fuji-san" ("Mt. Fuji") and written in Chinese by Jōzan Ishikawa (1583–1672), a former *samurai* retainer who had served Ieyasu Tokugawa. The silhouette of the sacred peak, which he was able to glimpse just as he was setting out on his journey, was a sight Morikami would never forget.

In general, immigrants were third-class passengers. For nearly the entire voyage they would remain belowdecks in the third-class passenger quarters, only once in a while going up on deck. Morikami, too, was a third-class passenger, but he became acquainted with a young Japanese on the ship who was in second class. By the end of the voyage they had become such close friends that they would meet on deck and shine each other's shoes. A young man from a wealthy family, Morikami's friend was going to England by way of North America to further his education. Two or three days before the ship reached Seattle, Morikami lost the sole from one of his shoes. The shoes were a purchase he had made just before boarding the ship in Kōbe. He had wasted two and a half *yen* of his money on the shoddily made goods. Had he looked at the shoes carefully before buying them, he could have seen that their soles were made of nothing more than pasteboard.

Morikami could go nowhere without shoes, and he knew no English. When his ship arrived in Seattle, he asked the youth in second class to buy him a new pair of shoes, which his friend did immediately upon disembarking. Morikami gave him the money for the purchase, but regretted doing so since he had so little. To top it off, the new shoes were too long and narrow. When Morikami tried them on, which he did with difficulty, he found around three inches of space in the toe. While trying to get them on, he caused them to flatten out in addition to being long and narrow. Morikami laughed because they looked like the gondolas he had seen in photographs of Venice, Italy. His introduction to America occurred amid confusion of this kind.

Seattle already had a lively community of Japanese immigrants. However, Morikami did not remain there long enough to learn about

American ways before boarding a train headed toward the Atlantic coast from the Pacific.

Starting with the California gold rush at the end of the 1840s, settlers seeking the so-called western frontier poured into the American West from east of the Mississippi. In order to provide access to the frontier, the building of railroads began on a large scale. The railroad system that was constructed had five routes crossing the continent as part of a vast railroad network that eventually connected every part of the country. As one of the five routes connecting the East and the West, the Great Northern Railroad began operation in 1893, with Seattle as its starting point on the Pacific coast. In cooperation with Nippon Yūsen Kaisha Steamship Company, the railroad served many passengers who were headed east from Seattle.

As a large-scale railroad system, the Great Northern Railroad crossed the Cascade Mountain Range and connected with cities in the Midwest such as St. Paul, Minnesota. Its construction was initially undertaken by Chinese laborers, but when Chinese immigration was halted, large numbers of Japanese were recruited to do the difficult work of clearing the land and leveling the terrain. Traveling the railroad that his country-men had in part built and thinking about the harsh environmental and working conditions they had endured, Morikami was jostled back and forth as he rode east and then south.

Plans for Japanese Immigration and the Development of Florida

The Rapid Expansion of the United States

During the century prior to the immigration of Sukeji Morikami and other Japanese to Florida, the United States was rapidly expanding. In 1803, it purchased the Louisiana Territory from France. It subsequently annexed Texas, then went to war with Mexico over disputed land along the Rio Grande River in the 1840s. With victory in this conflict, the US acquired additional Mexican territory that would become states, California, Arizona, and New Mexico included. In 1867 America purchased Alaska from Russia, and in 1898 it annexed Hawai'i.

After bringing the native population under control and opening the West to settlement, the United States expanded domestic markets first by crossing the continent with railroads and then by integrating the railroads into networks. The nation evolved from an agricultural to an industrial economy, surpassing even the developed nations of Europe. Corporations and trusts rapidly expanded, while captains of industry everywhere openly displayed their ostentatious material wealth.

Ceaseless immigration from Europe accompanied the United States' industrialization and westward expansion. Originally this flow of immigrants came from England, Germany, and other countries of northern and western Europe, but by the twentieth century an influx of individuals mostly from eastern and southern Europe had overtaken it.

Immigrants crossing the Atlantic Ocean entered New York harbor to be greeted by the sight of the Statue of Liberty. Brought to Ellis Island, they were processed through the facility there before being allowed entry into the United States. At the same time, immigrants also came from China, Japan, and other places on the other side of the Pacific Ocean. In the first decade of the twentieth century the number of immigrants entering the US from both Europe and Asia climbed to 8,790,000.

Newcomers did not confine themselves to the nation's urban centers, but sought out locales across the continent in which to settle. From the eastern US as well as from abroad, a constant stream of people wanting to establish new lives for themselves headed into the West, until then regarded as the frontier. By contrast, southern states such as Texas and Florida, both with low population densities, lagged behind in growth. For this reason the governments of both states actively sought foreign immigration in order to encourage development.

The Florida Peninsula as the Frontier

On a map of the United States, the Florida peninsula appears to be hanging beneath the southeastern section of the country. With the Gulf of Mexico on its west side and the Atlantic Ocean to the east, the peninsula extends southward toward the Caribbean Sea. From the tip of the peninsula, in a southwesterly direction, a chain of coral islands called the Florida Keys stretches like stepping-stones across nearly 150 miles before terminating in the island of Key West. From there, it is ninety-three miles to the island nation of Cuba.

Florida has an area similar to that of Japan if Hokkaidō is excluded. In the northern part of the state is a region of low hills, while the central and southern parts are almost entirely flat. At its highest point, Florida is no more than 345 feet above sea level.

Collecting water in the southern part of the state is Lake Okeechobee, the largest lake in the United States wholly within one state. South of the lake is the famous Everglades, a vast wetlands area that once occupied as much as 4,500 square miles. Farther south, in the islands off the end of the peninsula and in the Florida Keys, forests of mangroves grow along the shorelines.

Alligators, snakes, and lizards live in the slow-moving watercourses that meander through the state. Also seen in the clear water are manatees, the mammals that provided the model for the mermaid of legend. Pines as well as palms grow from the sandy soil, while saw palmettos cluster beneath them, their leaves divided into narrow, swordlike partitions arrayed in the shape of a fan.

No place is as eerie or as weird as Florida when moonlight shines on the crooked branches of oaks coiled in ivy and draped with Spanish moss resembling shredded rags. Mosquitoes, flies, and moths swarm everywhere. Once, swarming insects that attacked a group of barnyard animals were so thick that they choked a horse to death by flying into its nose and mouth—or so it is said. Finally, everything in the state is green and lush, and high humidity is a constant. Heavy rains and thunderstorms are regular visitors, as well as the occasional hurricane. This is what Florida is like.

The earliest inhabitants of the Florida peninsula, like all inhabitants of North America before the coming of the Europeans, were Indians. The first outsiders to set foot on the peninsula were a party of explorers led by the Spaniard Don Juan Ponce de León. They arrived in Florida in 1513 while exploring the nearby Bahama Islands for the purpose of establishing a colony by order of the Spanish king. Landing on the Atlantic coast in the middle of the peninsula, Ponce de León gave this land the name of La Florida. Colonization by the Spanish began in earnest at St. Augustine, founded in 1565. Under Spanish rule, St. Augustine was well established as a Catholic town with schools and churches decades before the Pilgrims arrived at Plymouth, Massachusetts, in 1620.

Afterward, possession of Florida changed several times. It was ceded to England for a time in 1763 as an outcome of the Seven Years' War in Europe (known as the French and Indian War in North America). Spain took possession of Florida a second time in 1783, but because of Spain's decline as a world power, it gave up all claims to the peninsula in 1821 when the United States took possession.

The number of Americans settling in Florida increased gradually. As this occurred, white settlers clashed with the peninsula's Native Americans, the Seminoles, and began applying pressure on the federal government to have them removed. The Seminoles opposed such efforts with armed resistance during a seven-year war starting in 1835. The result of the war was the relocation of many Seminoles west of the Mississippi River. Some of the few who remained withdrew into the vast wetlands of the Everglades. With these events as a background, Florida became the twenty-seventh state of the union in 1845.

In the national census of 1870, the distribution of Florida's population was as such:

Western region	9,478 people
Central region	15,779 people
Eastern region	8,956 people
Southern region	517 people

Dade County, which included the southern tip of the peninsula as well as the town of Miami not far north of it, had only eighty-five recorded inhabitants, all of whom surely hoped for the development of their underpopulated area.

Florida's leaders considered the establishment of agricultural colonies and the recruitment of settlers to be the most effective ways to develop their state. In the years following the Civil War, the government of Florida sought to recruit immigrants to the state by publicizing such selling points as the suitability of the soil for agriculture and the resolution of conflicts with the Seminoles. Moreover, Florida government officials wanting to match the state's development with that of Texas sought to entice settlers with public relations initiatives comparing Florida favorably with Texas. From the beginning, such recruitment efforts took a position that welcomed everyone from all parts of the country.

Moreover, immigration agents publicized Florida as a dream come true that was full of potential, using catchphrases like "Plenty of sunshine and warm weather." As a result of these efforts, agricultural enterprises began in several areas of the state. Among them were many that ended in failure, their stories differing considerably from those that promoters were publicizing.

In 1885, for example, fifty people came from Scotland to settle in Sarasota on the western side of the state. They purchased 6,000 acres through an agent, but when they reached their property for the first time, they found that its sandy soil made it unsuited to agriculture. Disappointed, most of the settlers abandoned the colony. In another similar instance, a group of Danes from the Midwest attempted to settle the community they called White City on Florida's Atlantic coast. The person acting as the agent for the colony enterprise pocketed the money from the sale of the land and disappeared. Although several settlers remained at the site, the agent's duplicity reduced them to poverty.

Despite experiences such as these, immigrants continued to respond to the promotions coming out of Florida. In the early twentieth century, immigrants from overseas and from other American states settled in Florida, especially its southern region where the peninsula remained undeveloped.

Jo Sakai, Student in New York

Even in Florida, where immigrants came from all over and were not stigmatized by where they were from, Jo Sakai's plan to introduce Japanese to the state was quite ambitious. It was unusual for Japanese immigrants possessing wealth and education to try carving out a utopian community in the United States. Examples of such efforts were known in Texas, but in Florida, with its great distance from Japan, Jo Sakai's colony project was the first of its kind. Sakai had the notion of creating an ideal colony based on his conviction that emigration was necessary for Japan. He knew that without it, the country's rapidly increasing population would overburden its natural resources.

Jo Sakai was born Kamosu Sakai on October 7, 1874, in the shadow of Miyazu Castle. He was the third son of Takamasu Sakai, a former retainer of the Miyazu Domain. By the time of Kamosu's birth, those relics of Japan's feudal past, the domains, had been abolished. Earlier, though, as the old era came to a close, Miyazu had sided with the outgoing regime, the Tokugawa Clan. In 1868, the first year of the Meiji Period, the Tokugawa suffered a defeat from the new imperial army at the Battle of Toba-Fushimi, in which Miyazu also participated.

Because of its support of the Tokugawa, the domain faced the likelihood of destruction by the imperial army sent to pacify the San'indō region where Miyazu was located. Instead, the domain demonstrated its allegiance with the new Meiji government by warmly welcoming

Gov.-Gen. Prince Kinmochi Saionji and allowing him to formally assume control. The eventual abolishment of all the domains resulted in
the establishment of prefectures throughout the country. For a short
time the former Miyazu Domain was part of Toyooka Prefecture, but
following a general reorganization of these political units, the central
government discontinued Toyooka and gave Kyōto Prefecture jurisdic-
tion over the domain's former territory instead.

Miyazu was in disastrous economic straits following the Meiji Restoration, and even the former *samurai* of the old Miyazu Domain, who
had lost their official status along with their stipends, were placed in an
untenable situation. Because the younger generation in particular had
nowhere to go for an education, uneasiness about their future increased.
Responding to the crisis, retainers of the former domain opened a private school in Miyazu, the Tenkyō Gijuku (Bridge of Heaven Academy), on July 1, 1875. The school's purpose was training future men of
ability.

The academy opened its doors five months prior to the opening of
another school in Kyōto Prefecture—Dōshisha English School, the
predecessor of present-day Dōshisha University—by Jō Niijima (1843–
90). A man named Seishu Sawabe, a teacher at the Tenkyō Gijuku, was
active in what became known as "the freedom and people's rights movement" (*jiyū minken undō*) that came into being at about this time. Thirteen years younger than Jō Niijima, Sawabe changed the character of
the Tenkyō Gijuku from a primarily educational institution to a people's rights association. It was one among several similar organizations
that sought to influence a movement to establish a national assembly,
and it supported the activities of the Constitution Party (Rikken Seitō),
which had been founded in Ōsaka. Sawabe enjoyed close friendships
with Jō Niijima and members of the Constitution Party.

Kamosu Sakai was eighteen years younger than Sawabe. He also had
connections with the Tenkyō Gijuku and Dōshisha through his father.
Takamasu Sakai was associated with the private academy in Miyazu by
means of his relationship with Sawabe, with whom he proposed forming a trading partnership called the Tenkyō Trading Company that was
to pursue business opportunities in Korea. Moreover, Takamasu was
a member of the Constitution Party. Kamosu watched how his father
conducted himself in business and participated in activities supporting

Jo Sakai at graduation from New York University, 1903 (courtesy Mori-kami Park and Japanese Gardens).

individual freedoms and ordinary people's rights. He was a powerful role model who influenced his son tremendously.

Soon Kamosu was enrolled in Dōshisha Normal School, another predecessor of the university that exists today. He attended Dōshisha, where he was imbued with Jō Niijima's training, from September 1894 to December 1896. Full of ambition, he then went to New York to further his education. There, he heard about development in Florida and the opportunities that were available in the state.

The number of people residing in New York City when Jo Sakai did had swelled with the influx of immigrants. Increasing from 120,000 people in 1820, New York City's population exceeded 3 million by the end of the nineteenth century. The city had also undergone rapid modernization. On Sixth Avenue the elevated railroad had begun running, and the subway was to be put into service by 1904. Carnegie Hall had been completed, mansions of the wealthy had appeared on Fifth Avenue, and beautiful luxury hotels had been constructed, beginning with the Waldorf Astoria. Department stores handling high-quality merchandise were open for business, while theaters and venues for other amusements, such as the circus, also flourished.

In contrast to this veneer of prosperity, European immigrants labored in the city's factories and lived in poverty side by side with others who had come from the same towns and villages in the old country. Especially in the slums of the Lower East Side, large families lived in small apartments and immigrant laborers struggled under wretched working conditions.

New York University stood where the two worlds of wealth and poverty met. While a student there, Sakai witnessed it all—the splendor created by the city's modernization and wealth as well as the effort necessary to climb out of poverty. In Union Square, only a few blocks from NYU, the author O. Henry began his career as a writer at just about this time. The city dwellers who provided the models for the characters in his short stories—stories that were rich with empathy for the human condition—lived all around Sakai. However, few Japanese living in New York were members of the working class like O. Henry's characters. Nearly all Japanese in New York at the time were either students, businesspeople, and people connected with government—the "upper crust" of society.

The earliest instance of Japanese visiting New York was that of the diplomatic mission of Masaoki Shinmi to ratify the US-Japan Treaty of Amity and Commerce negotiated by Townsend Harris in 1858. Shinmi and his entourage stayed in New York in 1860. In 1872 the mission of Tomomi Iwakura also visited as it sought treaty revisions in the US and Europe. In March of the same year, a Japanese consulate was established in the city.

In commerce, several business leaders soon established themselves in New York. Momotarō Satō and Toyo Morimura formed Hinode

Shōkai, a retail company dealing in miscellaneous Japanese goods that was a forerunner of the well-known porcelain importer Noritake. Ryōichirō Arai also joined with Satō to create the Satō-Arai Group, which traded in raw silk as well as curios and antiques. Japanese business enterprises that set up early branches in New York included the Yokohama Specie Bank and Mitsui Bussan.

Notable Japanese in the field of science also resided in New York at this time. One was Hideyo Noguchi (1876–1928), who worked as a principal research assistant at the Rockefeller Institute of Medical Research. Another scientist, Dr. Jōkichi Takamine (1854–1922), founded the Nippon Club in 1905 as a social center for the increasing number of expatriate Japanese living in the eastern United States.

As expatriate Japanese living in New York were on the increase, so were publications such as newspapers intended to serve the Japanese community. The weekly *Nichibei Shūhō*, called the *Japanese American Commercial Weekly* in English, was published by Hajime Hoshi and others starting in December 1900. By the end of the nineteenth century almost 300 Japanese resided in New York City. Social exchange within the Japanese community occurred not only through the Nippon Club but also through other similar institutions.

Jo Sakai enrolled in New York University's School of Commerce, Finance and Accounting on the island of Manhattan in the heart of New York City. Established in 1900, this school took as its mission the development of talented individuals as future business leaders. Large numbers of students sought to enter NYU's business school to study the areas of specialization identified in the institution's name. The school later became NYU's Stern School of Business and received high praise as one of the leading institutions of its kind in the United States.

Sakai, who probably called himself Jo by this time, attended NYU from 1902 to 1903, when he graduated. At the time, the enrollment fee was $5, while yearly tuition was $100. Adding miscellaneous and living expenses, the cost of his education at New York University may have amounted to as much as $1,000. This sum was twice the amount of the bonus that Morikami was promised in exchange for three years of work at the colony in Florida.

Consul General Uchida Lights a Fire

Even while Jo Sakai was a student at NYU, he was already looking into the possibility of establishing an agricultural colony somewhere in the United States. One person who had an impact on the colonization plans of Sakai and others was the Japanese consul general assigned to New York, Sadatsuchi Uchida. Uchida assumed the office of Japanese consul in New York in 1898, then served as consul general for nearly four years starting in 1902. When the Treaty of Portsmouth was negotiated at the conclusion of the Russo-Japanese War, he worked alongside Japanese foreign minister Jutarō Komura, the chief negotiator for the Japanese, to reach an equitable settlement with the Russians.

Uchida frequently visited different parts of the country while serving as consul general. He encouraged Japanese settlement in the US, especially Texas, by informing prospective settlers of the great potential there for agriculture. Second in area to Alaska among the American states, the vast, untouched wilderness of Texas extended inland from the shores of the Gulf of Mexico. At the beginning of the twentieth century, rice production prospered in Louisiana, the state neighboring Texas to the east. In Texas, too, the crop was found to be feasible, and a movement to encourage rice cultivation resulted through efforts in both the public and private sectors. Large development companies had land for rice production available in lots, and these entities wanted Japanese, who had a record of agricultural success on the West Coast, to acquire this land in Texas.

In 1902, when he was inspecting sites in the South to assess the potential for growing rice, Uchida accepted an invitation from the National Rice Growers Association to visit Beaumont, a city in the southeastern corner of Texas. While there, he spoke to his hosts about Japanese immigration to Texas, relating his vision of inviting independent, self-employed businessmen, rather than low-wage laborers, to the state.

Over the next several years, Uchida submitted a number of reports to the Japanese Foreign Ministry bearing such titles as "Rice Production in the Southern United States" (*"Hokubei Gasshūkoku Nanbu Shoshū ni Okeru Beisaku Jōkyō"*) and "The State of Rice-Growing in the American South" (*"Beikoku Nanbu Chihō Beisakugyō no Jōkyō"*). In them, Uchida explained the economic advantages for Japanese of cultivating rice in Texas, noting that the state's soil was fertile and, more importantly, that its land prices were far less expensive than Japan's. In contrast to the West Coast, Uchida reported, business enterprises could be established easily in Texas, where there was little anti-Japanese prejudice. The future was promising for those Japanese with wealth and education who immigrated to the state to cultivate rice. Conversely, he called attention to the fact that "poor, uneducated migrant [dekasegi] laborers" were unwelcome.

In Texas, then, where lots were being partitioned for sale as farmland, an atmosphere prevailed that favored settlement by Japanese who were skilled at rice farming. With the encouragement of the US Department of Agriculture, Uchida continued to promote Japanese immigration to Texas.

A report by the consul general appeared in a Japanese government publication, while the foreign ministry treated the topic of Japanese immigration to Texas in several reports of its own. Alongside such government publications was a constant outpouring of nonofficial immigration-related literature describing conditions and offering advice based on the experiences of settlers who had already established themselves in the state.

With articles of this kind appearing in Japan in the local press, talk of rice cultivation in Texas was on everyone's lips from one end of the country to the other. Eager to get a piece of the action, financiers and those with practical hands-on experience were soon heading toward the Great State of Texas. In this way, more than fifty Japanese started agricultural enterprises there in the space of only a few years following 1903.

Besides establishing farms in the Houston area, in the southern part of the state near the Gulf of Mexico, a number of Japanese settlers also had farms along the Rio Grande River, near the US border with Mexico. Some Japanese who started farming there did so after entering the US illegally from across the river. In this manner, the number of Japanese in Texas increased sharply in the early twentieth century, from as few as thirteen individuals in 1900, to 340 in 1910, and 449 in 1920.

A few options were available to the Japanese who wanted to farm in Texas. An immigrant could acquire land of his own to work himself or to lease out to another Japanese to work as a tenant. He could also lease land from a non-Japanese landowner to operate on a tenancy basis. From the beginning, though, most Japanese immigrants to Texas wanted to work for Japanese-owned enterprises already established in the state. This was the case for those coming directly from Japan and those coming from some other state of the union.

Several early Japanese landowners in Texas are worthy of note:

Yoshio Mayumi, who settled in Fannett, Texas, east of Houston. A prominent landowner in Mie Prefecture, Japan, he was a former member of the House of Peers, the upper house of the Japanese parliament.

Ichizō Kuki, who settled on the outskirts of Houston. He was the son of Ryūichi Kuki, first director general of the Japanese Imperial Museum, the predecessor of the Tōkyō National Museum. Ichizō Kuki was also the brother of Shūzō Kuki, a philosopher and the author of *Iki no Kōzō* (The Structure of *Iki*), a treatise on Japanese aesthetics.

Rihei Ōnishi, who went to Texas at the invitation of a relative. Previously a reporter for the influential Tōkyō daily newspaper *Jiji Shinpō*, he bought land south of Houston in the community of Webster.

Tōkyō native Junzō Hashimoto, who traveled with Ōnishi to the United States. He was the brother-in-law of Consul General Uchida.

Sadamatsu Takeda, from Kumamoto Prefecture in western Japan. He was a former corporate executive who had once been head of the Tientsin, China, branch of Mitsui Bussan.

The socialist Sen Katayama, who first left Japan for San Francisco in 1884 to study and work. He soon went on to Massachusetts, where he continued to work his way through school, then returned to Japan in 1896. Although he was busily involved in the labor movement, Katayama left Japan a second time in 1903 to grow rice in Texas. While in the US, he made contact with socialists and continued his involvement with the movement, running his rice-growing operation on the basis of socialist ideology.

Tsunekichi (Tom Brown) Okazaki was a Houston restaurant owner and Katayama's partner in their rice-growing enterprise. Okazaki entered the partnership committed to creating a wholly self-sufficient colony of Japanese in the manner of a Japanese village.

Other would-be entrepreneurs were attracted to the idea of forming large-scale agricultural operations, while still others hoped that rice farming in Texas would lead to a solution to Japan's problems of population size and food shortage. No matter what their motivation, such visionaries made plans that, while inspired, proved challenging for private investment, which bore all of the risk.

The Saibara Farm and Kishi Colony

Among these farming enterprises was one operated by the father-and-son team of Seitō and Kiyoaki Saibara, believed to be the most successful and enduring. Born in 1861 in a village that today is part of Tosa City in Kochi Prefecture, Japan, Seitō Saibara followed in the footsteps of Meiji Period elder statesman and Tosa City native son Taisuke Itagaki to become politically active in the freedom and people's rights movement. He was a lawyer and a politician who became a member of the lower house of the Japanese parliament in 1895. Having learned English at an early age, he was also a Christian, and in 1899 he accepted the position of fourth president of Dōshisha.

Saibara, who in 1903 was studying theology in Connecticut, read Uchida's report on rice farming and heard firsthand from Uchida himself. Determined to establish a farming operation in Texas, he acquired 300 acres of land in the vicinity of Webster, Texas, that same year. Preparing the irrigation system for wet rice agriculture, Saibara began cultivating the crop. Gradually he expanded his operation, trying out vegetables and cotton as well. In addition, he sold off his property in Japan and urged relatives to emigrate to Texas, where he himself intended to be buried as an American citizen.

Second only to Seitō Saibara as a person of means who operated a large-scale farm in Texas was Kichimatsu Kishi. Kishi settled in Terry, Texas, a town that exists today in name only, around sixty miles east of

Houston near Beaumont. From Nagaoka in Niigata Prefecture, Japan, he was born in 1871, putting him in the same generation as Jo Sakai. Kishi's grandfather was a prominent landowner, his father an entrepreneur with interests in oil and banking. He attended Tōkyō Commercial High School (forerunner of today's Hitotsubashi University), where he was a student when the Russo-Japanese War interrupted his studies. The imperial army sent Kishi to the front as a procurement officer acquiring supplies for the military.

After the war Kishi considered remaining in Manchuria to engage in agriculture but instead returned to Japan. He never gave up a desire to pursue business opportunities abroad, and he began to investigate locations overseas in which to settle. Indeed, he examined several locations that looked promising for rice cultivation, including South America and Australia.

After narrowing his search to the US, Kishi visited several states, beginning with California and including Louisiana, the Carolinas, and Mississippi, before finally settling on southeastern Texas. The deciding factors were the comparatively level terrain and the nearby source of water.

That being said, there were probably few other places in 1908 where 3,400 acres of unimproved farmland could be purchased for as little as $7,200. Kishi first recruited workers from Japan, sixteen in all. Some of them were laborers he employed, while the others leased his land as tenant farmers. Hitching up a mule, they prepared the ground for planting and irrigation of the paddies. Then the rice cultivation began.

A Yamato Colony on the Border with Mexico

Ten years after the establishment of Saibara's farm and the Kishi Colony, Japanese founded a similar venture on land near the mouth of the Rio Grande River and the US border with Mexico.

Sugarcane was an early crop raised in the Rio Grande Valley, or simply "The Valley," as this area was often called. In the early twentieth century, when the railroad was extended from Houston and irrigation became possible, farmers noticed that the land was good for growing vegetables as well. The first Japanese to begin farming this area came from other parts of Texas, later coming also from the West Coast and

Mexico. They established a farming enterprise that they called the Yamato Colony and operated on a cooperative basis.

In 1919, in the coastal town of Brownsville, Texas, seven Japanese men under the leadership of Minoru Kawahata from Kagoshima Prefecture, Japan, began operating their own farm. Since they had come to Texas separately, they decided to run the farm as a cooperative, unlike the ventures headed up by Saibara and Kishi. Kawahata had arrived in San Francisco in 1905. He had subsequently spent time in Denver, Colorado, and other places, moving to Texas after running a restaurant in Santa Fe, New Mexico.

The seven partners purchased approximately 400 acres of land that was already under cultivation as a sugar plantation. They hired between 50 and 100 laborers, and they raised several varieties of beans as well as potatoes and tomatoes amid European-style surroundings on a farm that had irrigation and a windmill.

At the time, this enterprise was being noticed by others in the region. But due to the poor quality of their land and the effects of the recession following World War I, the members of the association did not agree on how to handle problems that arose. Thus the partnership dissolved within as little as three years. Members distanced themselves from the business one by one, leaving Kawahata to deal with the colony's debts. He continued to farm, cultivating vegetables, cotton, and other crops, and shipped produce to market. Becoming a success, he benefitted the area and earned the community's considerable appreciation by constructing a church.

The California Yamato Colony

The Yamato Colony of Texas, then, existed briefly near the border with Mexico. In central California, immigrant Japanese established another colony bearing the name of Yamato near the small town of Livingston in 1906. It is probably the best-known of the agricultural communities named Yamato, and it was the special project of Kyūtarō Abiko, an important leader of the West Coast Japanese immigrant community.

Immigrant laborers from Japan spread out to all western states, where they took jobs in agriculture, as well as in the lumber, railroad, and fishing industries. As these workers' numbers increased, so did the backlash against them in white society. As a result, Japan and the United States entered into a "Gentlemen's Agreement" in 1908 limiting Japanese immigration to the US. In 1907, Executive Order 589 specifically prohibited the entry of Japanese laborers who made their way to the mainland United States by way of Hawai'i. Because of these developments, the departure from Japan by temporary migrant workers came to an end.

With such trends on the rise, some in the immigrant Japanese community began to reflect on the behaviors of their countrymen to identify the reasons behind the animosity toward them. Gambling, for example, was prevalent among laborers due to the rootlessness that many felt. From this reflection, leaders in the Japanese community began devising a plan to create an ideal colony that would give working-class Japanese in the United States the means and the opportunity to take up permanent residency in their adopted country.

Kyūtarō Abiko, who was the principal architect of the plan, was born in Suibara (today part of Agano City), Niigata Prefecture, Japan, in 1865. He developed an interest in America, was baptized as a Christian, and traveled to San Francisco in 1885. Abiko was a member of the Fukuinkai (Gospel Society), a Christian association affiliated with the Methodist Church and organized by Japanese in San Francisco. Sponsored by the Fukuinkai, he attended the University of California and later became the association's head. As the number of students and other disfranchised Japanese living from one day to the next in the US grew, he began to consider ways in which to improve their lives.

In October 1902, Abiko set up a company to negotiate labor contracts for Japanese workers. At the time, immigrant laborers were increasing in number, and so was the demand for Japanese labor. Abiko was able to expand his firm, which he incorporated as the Japanese Industrial Company (Nihon Kangyōsha) in 1904.

As a way to develop real estate, Abiko considered using Japanese Industrial Company funds to finance an agricultural colony that would be populated by Japanese settlers. Deciding on a site near Livingston in central California, the company first purchased 1,280 acres of land, subdivided it, and sold it in lots to those wanting to settle. Abiko called his settlement the Yamato Colony, and he recruited Japanese colonists for it through advertisements in Japanese-language newspapers, including his own, the *Nichibei Shinbun*. The first settler, Tajirō Kishi, originally from Wakayama Prefecture, came in 1906, the same year that George Morikami arrived in Florida. Two years later, in 1908, thirty colonists occupied Abiko's Livingston settlement.

The Yamato colonists began raising their crops on an arid, desert-like tract, but before long they were successfully harvesting eggplants, sweet potatoes, asparagus, tomatoes, and other produce despite the poor soil conditions. Colony members worked cooperatively, beginning with buying and selling provisions and building a packinghouse.

Henry Morrison Flagler: Ambitions of a Wealthy Developer

At the time that the Yamato Colony was established in California, over 6,800 Japanese immigrants resided in Los Angeles alone. In comparison, and according to the 1910 US Census, the number of Japanese living in Texas was 340, and the number in Florida was not more than 50.

However, in Texas and Florida there was a potential for development that the West Coast lacked. Consul General Uchida's report on Texas seemed to encourage Jo Sakai, who lived in New York. Seitō Saibara also lived there at this time, and Sakai was probably acquainted with this former president of Dōshisha, the Kyōto school that Sakai had once attended. He could well have been receiving information and advice from Saibara. From this, it is only natural to surmise that Sakai, too, probably considered going to Texas. He may have considered Florida a possible location for a colonization project due to the connection between Florida and New York University, where Sakai was a student.

Around the time that development began in Florida, a development firm called the Model Land Company was established. Company president James Ingraham was a friend of Joseph French Johnson, a dean at New York University, which Sakai was attending. Ingraham was aware of the successes in agriculture already shown by Japanese immigrants in California. Based on this knowledge, he conceived the notion of having Japanese settle in Florida and develop the state agriculturally. He may have shared this idea with Professor Johnson, who in turn told Sakai about it.

By this time, the Florida East Coast Railway (FECR) extended along the Atlantic coast of Florida from Jacksonville in the north to Miami in the south. The Model Land Company, a subsidiary of the FECR, was

Map of the peninsula of Florida published by the Florida East Coast Railway (courtesy Henry Morrison Flagler Museum).

formed to handle the development of land on either side of the railroad tracks. Placing Ingraham in charge of the Model Land Company was the founder of the FECR, Henry Morrison Flagler. He was already known as one of the wealthiest men in America.

Born in upstate New York in 1830, Henry Flagler left school at the age of fourteen and went to work in the grain business, where he eventually met John D. Rockefeller. Taking advantage of rapid growth in the oil refining industry, Rockefeller established an oil refining business in which Flagler joined him as a partner. In 1870 Standard Oil was born.

In 1878, Flagler, who late in life possessed a fortune worth many millions of dollars, visited Jacksonville for the sake of his wife's health, which had long been poor. Although she passed away in 1881, Flagler visited Florida again two years later. Together with his second wife he made a short visit to St. Augustine, the town south of Jacksonville that had been built by the Spanish who had landed there in the sixteenth century.

Both husband and wife were pleased with the region's climate. From his experience in St. Augustine, Flagler became convinced that Florida held tremendous potential for the development of first-class seaside resorts much like those of the Riviera, and he decided to begin developing them himself. First he opened a luxurious hotel in St. Augustine, the Ponce de León, that boasted 450 guest rooms and lavish décor. He then purchased a railroad already operating in the St. Augustine area and extended its tracks southward, rechristening it the Florida East Coast Railway. At the same time, Flagler moved his development of resort facilities southward.

The most iconic of the resorts developed by Flagler was at Palm Beach. In 1894, he opened a colonial-style 540-room hotel called the Royal Poinciana on the narrow barrier island that boasted of a long beach. At the time the world's largest wooden building, the Royal Poinciana faced the Lake Worth Lagoon and was elegantly surrounded by palm trees. A few years after its completion, Flagler added on to the hotel, making it even more resplendent. With a height of six stories, it had over 1,100 guest rooms and extended from north to south for nearly half a mile. The hotel was a magnificent architectural feat constructed on an unbelievable scale.

Henry Morrison Flagler (courtesy Florida State
Archives).

To serve hotel guests, Flagler built a pier that stretched 300 yards
into the ocean. A steamship picked up passengers from this pier and
carried them on sightseeing excursions to Nassau in the Bahama Islands
and Cuba. Flagler put up another nearby hotel overlooking the ocean; it
became known as The Breakers. In this way, he made early Palm Beach
a world-class resort.

Even in his private life Flagler pushed the limits of extravagance by
building a winter residence for his wife in Palm Beach. Whitehall, as he
called his mansion, was a chalk-white palace with a facade of marble pil-
lars and a roof of red tiles.

In his eagerness to keep on developing, Flagler did not know where
to stop. He extended his railroad another sixty miles south to Miami,
where he built even more hotels. Even while workers laid new track,

well-heeled patrons came in a constant stream, traveling in extravagantly appointed Pullman cars to visit the playgrounds in Florida that he had created for them.

When Flagler decided to extend his railroad and develop tourism across the chain of islands that was the Florida Keys all the way to Key West, he may have believed that he was fulfilling his destiny. On the other hand, the US government had just begun construction of the Panama Canal that was to open a shipping route linking the Atlantic and Pacific Oceans.

Flagler's plans for the railroad were tied to the opening of the Panama Canal. Since Key West had a reasonably large population and was situated on a deep-water harbor, it would make the ideal terminus for a lucrative shipping route between Florida and the canal. A Key West terminus would also stimulate trade with Latin America, particularly Cuba. With this fact in mind, Flagler conceived his ambitious plan to build an "overseas railroad" that would connect the coral islands of the Keys like beads on a string.

During the time he spent with Standard Oil, Flagler was ruthless in his business dealings and would go to almost any length to achieve his goals. In contrast, he seemed to take an approach to Florida's development that was more inclusive and socially aware. He encouraged the public to come to the state to settle communities of their own making that would maintain his railroad's profitability through their commercial activities. Jo Sakai's colony project was part of a wave of development resulting from Flagler's approach. It was Sakai's good fortune and fortuitous timing that allowed him to ride the crest of this wave.

Flagler's expectations were not simply for the development of resorts, but also for growth to take place on the land on either side of the railroad tracks. He hoped to see these properties developed agriculturally and managed with an enterprising spirit. To encourage experimentation with new crops and farming methods, Flagler often provided financial assistance through loans to settlers who needed them.

The government of Florida welcomed such plans and enacted legislation granting a certain number of acres of land to the railroads, beginning with Flagler's, for every mile of railroad track they laid. In accordance with this legislation, the FECR claimed more than 2 million acres of land. In this way, then, Flagler's organization took charge of the development of vast tracts of land through which the railroad passed. The Model Land Company, a subsidiary of the FECR, managed the railroad's real estate holdings under the guidance of its president, James Ingraham, a man who had been with the railroad for many years. He was also the person placed in charge of the colony established by Jo Sakai and his settlers.

The Founding of
Florida's Yamato Colony

Jo Sakai Tours the Florida Peninsula in Search of a Colony Site

Recently graduated from New York University, Jo Sakai took steps in November 1903, to advance his proposal for establishing a Japanese colony in the United States, a project about which he felt passionate. He hoped to make a round of possible colony sites in the eastern US, particularly in Florida, and then return to Japan to recruit settlers.

Sakai headed first to Jacksonville, Florida's largest city, to evaluate how receptive Floridians would be to his colony project and to begin the search for a possible colony site. From New York he took the steamship *Arapahoe*. The elegant passenger liner with masts fore and aft and a smokestack between them could accommodate well over a hundred passengers. As probably the only Japanese on board, Sakai sailed south, arriving in Jacksonville on November 17.

According to the US Census, only one Japanese resided in the state of Florida in 1900. There may have been others who were not counted, but most likely no students or laborers. If there had been other Japanese, they probably would have been businessmen in the state's urban centers. However, in one unusual case, a Japanese did live for a short time in Jacksonville in April 1891. He was the unconventional scholar Kumagusu Minakata, who later became famous as a botanist. Minakata studied botany and other subjects while living in Ann Arbor, Michigan, although he never enrolled in the University of Michigan. Hearing that Florida held a treasure trove of lichens, Minakata traveled to Jacksonville in order to collect them. He stayed in the Florida city for a time before moving on to Cuba.

Jo Sakai's own visit to Jacksonville occurred almost eleven years after Minakata's departure. Sakai, who carried with him letters of introduction from Joseph Johnson, the dean of the business school at New York University, called on Charles E. Garner, president of the Jacksonville Board of Trade. The board could open doors for him in state government and the business community. With an introduction from Garner, Sakai would be able to meet with officials of the Florida East Coast Railway (FECR), to whom he hoped to present his plan for a Japanese agricultural colony in Florida.

The *Florida Times-Union*, a Jacksonville newspaper, reported on Sakai's visit and the interest in his colony plan among business leaders. The paper also devoted space to the man himself, describing Sakai's behavior and character in an article that appeared in the paper two days after the Japanese entrepreneur's arrival. "An effort is being made to bring a colony of Japanese settlers to Florida by Mr. J. Sakai, who arrived in the city Tuesday morning on the steamer *Arapahoe*," the article began. It reported that Sakai was from Kyōto, Japan, had studied at Dōshisha, and was a graduate of New York University. In addition, the article's writer emphasized that Sakai had come bearing glowing letters of recommendation.

The reporter wrote both of Sakai's purpose for establishing the colony and the principles behind it, stating, "Mr. Sakai . . . is a man with a purpose, and that purpose is not one of self-emolument. One needs but to talk with him to be convinced that something higher and nobler than . . . pecuniary profit inspires him to seek a location for a colony of his countrymen in America."

The *Times-Union* article then quoted Sakai himself, first expressing his observations of Florida. "Your climate is like that of the southern part of Japan. My people would experience no inconvenience or illness from the change. I have not yet examined your soil, but I believe that it is adapted to the cultivation of rice and tea." About his motive for starting the colony project and his intentions, Sakai spoke to the reporter as follows:

> The resources of my own country are not adequate to the largely increasing population. Emigration from Japan is a necessity. Within the past thirty-six years there has been an emigration of 50,000 to the Hawaiian islands. What is the result? Japanese predominate in the population of the islands. Chinese rank next in number, the native population next in order, mixed and Portuguese. The export products of Japan are silk, tea and matting. It is my purpose to start first a rice plantation; next a tea orchard, and then to take up the silk industry. This can all be done in Florida successfully.

Cordially received by the business community of Jacksonville, Sakai next visited St. Augustine, a short ride to the south by rail. Here, in the oldest city in the United States remained the ambiance of Spanish colonial Florida, embodied in the old stone fort that overlooked the harbor and the narrow streets lined with antiquated buildings. Here also were brand-new luxury hotels, which had given Flagler his toehold in the future development of Florida. This city that took pride in its past was where the Model Land Company maintained its headquarters.

In St. Augustine, Sakai met with Model Land Company president James Ingraham. Sakai, through Dean Johnson, already had received an invitation from Ingraham to settle his colony on land owned by the FECR. But Sakai was not certain that the railroad or the Model Land Company had the best deal to offer him. Rather, the purpose of his meeting with Ingraham was merely to hear the terms of any agreement that the two men might sign.

Sakai did not inspect railroad-owned land immediately. Instead, he headed west across the Florida peninsula to the state capital at Tallahassee, then to Leon County, where Tallahassee was located and where other potential offers awaited him. He met with state governor William S. Jennings, whom he asked for support and cooperation regarding the colony project.

Governor Jennings greeted his foreign visitor warmly. Handing the governor the letter of introduction that Dean Johnson had written for him, Sakai laid out his plans for establishing a colony of Japanese in Florida. Jennings penned another letter of introduction on Sakai's behalf briefly describing the Japanese entrepreneur's plans and indicating his own support of them. He believed the entire state would support Sakai's project. "[The] procurement of a Japanese Colony of a deserving class of the Japanese people," Jennings wrote, "would be highly approved by the people of Florida." Sakai's reception in Jacksonville and the state capital could only be described as highly encouraging. On the basis of his treatment by the state's political and business leaders, then, Sakai committed himself to locating his colony in Florida rather than in Texas.

Sakai inspected several locations in Leon County that had been offered to him as sites for his colony outside of the state capital. One site was owned by a prominent local citizen, but he hoped to settle Sakai's proposed colonists as tenant farmers, and intended only to lease land to them with no thought of ever transferring its ownership.

In the same area, a clergyman named E. Warren Clark appealed to Sakai with an offer to locate the colony on the farmland he owned. Clark was familiar with Japan, having first visited the country in the 1870s at the invitation of Kaishū Katsu, a prominent statesman not only in the government of the *shōgun* but in the reform-minded government of the emperor that followed it. An educator as well as a clergyman, Clark taught English, history, science, and other subjects at the Shizuoka Gakumonjo, a school in Shizuoka, Japan, founded originally for the benefit of the *samurai* retainers of the Shizuoka Domain, who were also vassals of the *shōgun*. Clark later taught physics and chemistry at Tōkyō Kaisei Gakkō, the forerunner of present-day Tōkyō University, where he briefly mentored pioneering Japanese educator Masanao Nakamura.

Returning to the United States after four years in Japan, Clark wrote a book about his experiences there titled *Life and Adventure in Japan*. Several years later he arrived in Tallahassee, where he acquired a farm he called the Shidzuoka [*sic*] Plantation due to his years of living in Shizuoka, Japan. He was already raising such Japanese crops as tea, cotton, mulberries, and persimmons, and he boasted the largest acreage in the county devoted to corn.

Clark explained his preparations to receive Sakai and his group with enthusiasm: "My knowledge of the Japanese people, language, and customs would enable me to be of great assistance to you. This is a better State for [Japanese] than Texas. Better also than Hawaii. . . . I could house a dozen Japanese families here at once if I only had them."

But once again Clark's proposal did not include the transfer of property ownership to the colonists. It did not fit Sakai's plan to create a colony in which members would own their own land. A few other proposals were tendered in Leon County, and Sakai investigated them as well. Afterward, he headed south along the Gulf of Mexico on the western side of the state. Arriving in the city of Tampa, Sakai continued on to Manatee County, then farther south to Lee County, coincidentally the location of the winter residence of Thomas Edison whom Sakai greatly admired. In both counties Sakai had received inducements to settle his colonists, and he inspected several possible colony sites.

After visiting Tallahassee and Florida's west coast, Sakai increasingly regarded land owned by the FECR at Boca Raton, situated on the Atlantic Ocean side of the state, as the most likely location for the colony. From Lee County, he retraced his steps, first heading north, and then crossing Florida to Jacksonville. From there, the Florida East Coast Railway ran in a straight line through St. Augustine and southward along the Atlantic coast.

According to local legend, Spanish pirates had long ago buried their treasure of gold doubloons and other valuables in the Boca Raton area. Before pirates haunted the local waters, though, an indigenous people called the Tequesta had lived there. Beginning in the 1500s, Spanish slave traders captured many of these Indians and sold them as slaves in Cuba and elsewhere in the West Indies. Other Tequesta died of diseases introduced by the Europeans. Finally, the Spanish removed many of them at the time of their own expulsion from Florida when the British assumed control of the peninsula. In this way the aboriginal population, remaining in only a few scattered groups, had been erased from memory.

Afterward, Native Americans migrating from Alabama and Georgia formed the Seminole tribe and spread throughout Florida, including the Boca Raton area. From the time that the United States took possession of Florida in 1821, though, the number of white settlers on the peninsula increased, leading to conflicts and demands to the government that the Seminoles be removed. At the conclusion of the Second Seminole War, they had mostly been expunged.

With the removal of nearly all of the Indians from Florida, no one lived in the Boca Raton area for several decades. Setting foot there for the first time in a long while was a surveyor and civil engineer from Ohio named Thomas Rickards. Rickards saw the Boca Raton area while traveling around the Florida peninsula as a surveyor for the state and was impressed. In 1892 he settled there in a house he built beside the canal that was to become the Intracoastal Waterway. As Boca Raton's first settler, Rickards began cultivating oranges and pineapples, but his fields sustained considerable damage from a hurricane. At the same time, Flagler was laying tracks for the FECR through Boca Raton. He hired Rickards as an agent for the Model Land Company to sell property in the area that the railroad owned.

Rickards took charge of handling the sales of property to farming families who would then use the railroad to ship their produce to markets in the north. Sakai, who was hoping to bring an entire colony of farmers to the area, was certainly a customer to whom Rickards felt he ought to pay attention. In December 1903, Rickards received a telegram from Model Land Company president James Ingraham informing him that the colony organizer would soon arrive. He met Sakai, who was traveling from St. Augustine, at the Boca Raton train station.

Welcomed into Rickards's home, Sakai inspected properties in the area and spoke with his host at length about prospects there for the proposed colony. Rickards's neighbor Frank Chesebro, who had settled in the area and started cultivating pineapples after Rickards, recorded Sakai's movements in his diary:

December 25, 1903: A Jap here at Rickard's [sic] looking for a tract of land for a colony.

Two days later this entry followed:

December 27, 1903: Mr. Curry and the Jap leaving on the train.

Completing his inspection of properties in the Boca Raton area, Sakai returned to Jacksonville, where he had first set foot in Florida.

The train in which he rode headed north by way of St. Augustine across Florida's flat terrain and beside its white, sandy beaches. He had covered as many miles in Florida as he would have had he traveled the circumference of Honshū, Japan's main island.

Sakai had traveled all over Florida in search of a site for his proposed colony. Returning to Jacksonville, he was approached once again by a reporter for the *Florida Times-Union* eager to learn how his plans were progressing. "Sakai's idea is to bring over about forty families to begin with," the newspaper explained, "and he will locate four colonies, ten families to the colony." The year 1903 was nearly at an end.

On the last day of the year, Sakai started out from Jacksonville for his home in New York. On the way, he stopped in Washington, DC, to meet with officials of the US Department of Agriculture and the Bureau of Immigration. The outcome of these meetings could not have been more positive. Both offices supported his proposal.

With the question of the colony's location nearly settled, and having received the enthusiastic encouragement of both the people of Florida and the federal government, Sakai's plan had easily cleared a couple of potential stumbling blocks. The next problem was the practical one of recruiting colonists willing to make the long journey to Florida.

Once he had returned to New York, Sakai shared his feelings about setting up the colony in a letter to Thomas Rickards dated February 1, 1904. "I am still living under [the] dusty air of New York," he wrote, "[and] dreaming [of] my future house in Fla."

The Effects of the Russo-Japanese War

In February 1904, Sakai departed for Japan to recruit settlers for the colony, at the same time dispatching to Florida a relative by the name of Nobuji Inouye. Inouye, who also happened to be living in New York, was twenty-three years old. Born Nobuji Tanaka, he had been adopted into the Inouye household as heir. The Tanaka household into which he had been born was that of a village headman near Mineyama on the Tango Peninsula. The Inoue family was the wealthiest in the district.

Departing from New York, Sakai traveled to Montreal, Canada, and from there crossed the continent by rail. As his train left for Vancouver, it encountered heavy snowfall that delayed his arrival and caused him to worry that he would miss his connection. Nevertheless, he sailed for Japan on time. He contacted Rickards through an associate in New York, learning that Inouye had arrived in Boca Raton without mishap.

It took Sakai until the middle of March, more than a month, to reach his hometown of Miyazu. In the meantime the Russo-Japanese War had broken out. From Kyōto, Sakai sent Rickards a letter on March 16:

> As you know, our country is exciting all over for the war but I am hoping it will be settled very soon. I am quite busy . . . entertain[ing] many visitors who want [to] know the news of U.S. every day. I may stay in this city [a] few weeks more to make out [a] report of our colonization plan [in the] Japanese language and I will call [on] our government in our Capital City. . . . Present Japanese are very small in every manners and I am feeling very uncomfortable to live in [a] Japanese house even [though] I [was] born [in] such a place.

Sakai concluded his letter on an upbeat note. "How I love [the] U.S. you can not guess it!" he wrote. The letter, which was intended to reassure Rickards, strongly implied that the outbreak of the Russo-Japanese War would have no effect on the colony project. Despite Sakai's optimism, Model Land Company president James Ingraham expressed his reservations in a letter to Rickards dated April 5. "I am very much afraid that the war is going to interfere with Mr. Sakai's plans. I do not believe that the authorities would permit any number of families to leave during a state of warfare, when they might require every able-bodied individual," he wrote. Ingraham had signed a contract with Sakai. The Model Land Company president and other supporters of the colony project were concerned that settlers recruited by Sakai might not make it to Florida to fulfill the contract's terms.

In a letter to Rickards dated April 27, Sakai detailed how busy he was negotiating with the Japanese Foreign Ministry while consulting with backers of the project. The news was not altogether good:

> I am almost all ready to select our colonizers . . . but our Foreign Department of government is strongly opposed to giv[ing] the passports to our people for U.S. . . . Since [a] few years ago, our government has [stopped sending] out our people for U.S. [on]

account [of the] labor unions interfer[ring with] our immigrations.

I believe it is the principle [sic] reason . . . against my claim to have passports [for] our colonizers and never . . . our trouble with Russia.

Although Sakai had told the *Times-Union* reporter that he intended to bring "forty families" from Japan, gathering a group of that size proved difficult. Sakai did select a number of participants for the colony project while also lining up funding for it, and he wanted the foreign ministry to grant the permission necessary for these colonists to travel abroad as quickly as possible. To achieve this outcome, he and his associate in New York, K. Miyachi, tried appealing to government leaders in Japan as well the consul general posted to New York.

In Japan, Sakai drew on personal connections to try to influence Foreign Minister Jutarō Komura and bring him around to the point of view of the colony organizers. To accomplish this, he recruited the assistance of other members of the cabinet of Prime Minister Tarō Katsura, individuals such as Minister of Agriculture and Commerce Keigo Kiyoura, to speak on behalf of Sakai's project. Komura only repeated to these colleagues that he would take up the matter of passports for the colonists as soon as the international situation allowed it.

Sakai also sought the assistance of Shigenobu Ōkuma, even though the political party headed by this influential leader, the Kenseihontō, was not currently in power. Obtaining an introduction from a veteran member of the Japanese House of Representatives, Tomotsune Kōmuchi, Sakai met with Ōkuma. Kōmuchi, who made the meeting possible, hailed from the Tango Peninsula. He had represented the Imperial Household Agency at the Philadelphia Exposition of 1876 and later served in the second cabinet of Masayoshi Matsukata as chief cabinet secretary. Ōkuma understood Sakai's predicament with regard to the colony plan and the matter of passports. He told Sakai that his party members would put the question before the foreign affairs committee of the Imperial Diet as a political issue.

In the meantime, K. Miyachi was in New York taking care of matters related to the colony effort there while Sakai was in Japan. Miyachi met with Consul General Sadatsuchi Uchida to explain the colony proposal and ask him to intercede on the project's behalf before the foreign ministry. After meeting with Uchida at least once, Miyachi wrote to Rickards requesting that he ask attorneys among his acquaintances whether they could provide written opinions regarding the legal rights of Japanese immigrants in Florida. Believing Uchida wanted reassurances, Miyachi submitted to the consul general statements from both former West Palm Beach mayor George Currie and the attorney for the Model Land Company.

Miyachi, however, found that Uchida did not react favorably to the comments tendered by the attorneys in Florida. As a result, Ingraham angrily charged that Uchida was unable to throw his support behind the Florida project because of favoritism toward Japanese colonies in Texas. He was well aware that Uchida had a hand in expanding rice production in Texas and encouraging the settlement of Japanese immigrants there.

The Colonists Arrive from Japan

As no progress was being made in the situation concerning the passports, Sakai hit on an ingenious plan. Since the Japanese government had a policy of encouraging the study abroad of Western technical skills and business practices, he would have the colony members travel overseas as students. If all colonists applied for and obtained their own passports, they would disguise their true purpose, that of establishing a permanent agricultural colony.

Whether it was the result of this strategy or not, the colonists' passports were issued without further problem. Sakai was relieved. Although Japanese immigrants to the United States had been issued passports as farm laborers in the past, he had worried that openly consulting government officials and politicians about the colony project would leave his group without passports. Moreover, it might exacerbate the problem by stirring up anti-Japanese sentiment against him in the US.

Instead, the first of the colonists left Japan individually to make their way to Florida. By mid-August, 1904, two additional colonists had joined Nobuji Inouye at the site of the future colony. Sakai and several other Japanese on their way to the Sunshine State disembarked in San Francisco in November. Ingraham, who was aware that they were coming, met them in Jacksonville and had Rickards make the necessary preparations for their arrival in Boca Raton. Sakai himself was delayed when his trunk was left behind in Jacksonville and he had to return there to claim it. He arrived in Boca Raton after the others on November 26.

Writing to Rickards, Ingraham informed him, "I have told [Sakai] . . . that you had lands that you would let [the Japanese] have at a fair rental . . . on which they could make an experimental crop this season, under your direction and thus obtain experience and expert knowledge." Ingraham also shared Sakai's response: "He tells me the young men are much pleased with the prospect and that a good many more will come as soon as permitted."

Once Sakai arrived, the Japanese began to organize themselves as a colony. For the time being, they would cultivate land rented from Rickards. Ingraham and Rickards provided the colonists with housing, tools, and fertilizer. They also had the fields cleared in preparation for planting in order to help the newcomers "make a living out of the crop." Ingraham provided advice when Sakai consulted with him, which he did early on about acquiring a horse and wagon for transporting the colonists' harvest at the end of the season. Ingraham advised Sakai to "not make the mistake of spending money that is not . . . necessary."

His manner in explaining his position to Sakai seemed like scolding. "You have a party of young men with you who are agricultural students," he told the colony leader. He continued as follows:

They came here without means; they wish to make an experimental test of vegetable growing this season upon the most economical plan possible in order that they may derive experience and practice from it that will enable them to successfully establish and conduct farms of their own for both fruit and vegetable growing. To do this successfully, they must start on an economical basis and carry on their work just as other young men do, (Americans) who under the same circumstances work out their own success.

Sakai, who usually followed Ingraham's advice, was generally satisfied with the arrangements that had been made for his settlers. Indeed, plans for the colony progressed as they did because the two men enjoyed such a good relationship. Inevitably, some problems did occur. But while Rickards procured the tools and supplies that Sakai and his colonists considered to be necessary, ultimately it was the Model Land Company that managed the colony's accounts, by the terms of its contract with Sakai. Sometimes disagreements arose between the company and the colonists as to what was deemed necessary and what was not.

The matter of the horse and wagon was one such instance. Sakai felt that a horse and wagon were essential to farmwork and wanted to purchase them. Ingraham, on the other hand, thought that hiring a horse and wagon when needed was more economical. Taking into consideration the cost of the animal's care, he could not agree to the purchase of the two items. In the end the parties agreed to leave the decision to Rickards. Out of respect for Sakai's point of view and considering the feelings of the young men that a horse was not merely a means of transportation, Rickards approved the purchase.

At the same time, something else was happening that troubled Ingraham: Once the presence of Sakai and his Japanese colonists had become widely known, others began showing up with offers to sell them property. Against such opportunists, Ingraham warned Sakai and Rickards to take precautions.

Curiosity about the Newcomers

While the first colonists made preparations to plant their experimental crop, additional settlers from Japan trickled in one by one. By the end of 1904, they numbered nearly twenty individuals. These included Mitsusaburo Oki, who was the sponsor of the colony enterprise as well as Sakai's brother-in-law; Tamemasu (Henry) Kamiya, Sakai's younger brother who had been adopted by the Kamiya family of Hokkaidō as heir to the family name; Nobuji Inouye, who was the first of the colony members to come to Florida; and Aisuke Tsujii. Those who came from Kyōto or the Tango Peninsula area were almost all prominent men in their respective communities who possessed some personal wealth.

Others associated with the colony effort were K. Miyachi and Tokusaburo Inaho, who were already in New York, and Masakuni Okudaira, who remained in the United States after graduating from Yale University. Okudaira was the second son of Masayuki Okudaira, the last *daimyō*, or regional lord, of the Nakatsu Domain on Japan's southernmost main island of Kyūshū. His older brother, head of the family

Masayasu Okudaira, held the title of count and was a member of the House of Peers, the upper house of the Japanese parliament. Masakuni also used the title of count. Born in 1880, he was a student at the Nakatsu Middle School before graduating to the Peers' School in Tōkyō. In January 1904, he enrolled at Yale University.

Okudaira, a friend of Dr. Jōkichi Takamine, the eminent chemist who was also a founder of the Nippon Club in New York, recognized the potential for agriculture in Florida. He approved of Sakai's proposal for a Japanese agricultural colony there, and he considered joining the venture as a settler and investing in it.

In Japan, the Okudaira family called on individuals from its old domain in Nakatsu, Ōita Prefecture, to join the colony effort in Florida. It made one of the mansions in Tōkyō that it had owned since feudal times into a kind of gathering place for prospective colonists before they undertook the voyage to America. Masakuni's approach to the colony effort was that of a manager of a business enterprise who invested funds and hired employees. With his powerful physical presence and his nobleman's title, local newspapers erroneously reported that he was a member of the Japanese imperial family.

Among the colonists were several who were able to speak English and Spanish, including Sakai. Rickards was effusive in his praise of them. They were different from the usual immigrant, he told the press. They were intelligent, hardworking, quick to learn, and possessed of a certain refinement resulting from a cultured upbringing. "Clean of body and clear of mind," Rickards said of the colonists, "they are the best living examples of temperate and energetic manhood I have ever seen." Compared to these early settlers, one might feel that Morikami, who joined the colony later, might not have measured up.

On Christmas Eve, Rickards invited the Japanese to his house for a party. George Currie showed up as the festivities got under way. The former mayor of West Palm Beach sang Sakai and the others a song in Japanese that was the hit of the party.

On January 1, 1905, the Japanese colonists gathered at the packinghouse to celebrate the "year 2565," counting from the reign of the mythical first emperor, Jimmu Tennō. A number of Americans from the neighborhood, including Frank Chesebro, dropped by and had supper with the Japanese. The colonists sang Japanese songs and demonstrated *sumō*, providing an introductory lesson in Japanese culture for their guests.

In February, the Japanese colonists began harvesting the tomato crop on which they had begun their training, to good results. Observing the Japanese newcomers and seeing how hard they worked, the people of Boca Raton were concerned for their welfare and lent them a willing hand when the necessity arose. In one instance, the Japanese had to dig up several scrub palmettoes, a plant with an extensive system of tough, hard-to-remove roots, in order to clear land for cultivation. The tenacious plants confounded the colonists' best efforts to remove them until Frank Chesebro, something of a mentor to the colonists, lent them the use of a stump-removal machine. Chesebro often assisted in other ways as well.

At the time, a movement opposing Japanese immigration was underway in California and elsewhere in the West, leading to the formation of the Asiatic Exclusion League in San Francisco in 1905. Japan's dominance in the Russo-Japanese War, which was seen as a threat to the West Coast, became a prime factor in the rise of anti-Japanese sentiment there. In southern Florida, though, such a problem did not exist. Captain Garner, president of the Jacksonville Board of Trade, criticized American labor unions' support of Japanese exclusion, saying that it put the United States, and especially Florida, at a disadvantage. Recognizing the importance of Sakai's colony project to the state, Garner publically defended Japanese immigration to the US.

On March 17 Consul General Uchida came by rail from New York to see for himself conditions at the colony. When Uchida concluded his visit, Sakai accompanied him as far as Jacksonville on his way back to New York. There Capt. Garner and others who favored Sakai's colony enterprise entertained the consul general with a banquet, which was attended even by William S. Jennings, at that point the former state governor.

In an address before the banquet's guests, Uchida acknowledged that the colonists at Boca Raton appeared to be doing well. He told his audience that the Japanese government was "very particular" about who should leave the country. In addition, he indicated that the question of whether additional settlers would be allowed to immigrate depended on how likely they were to succeed. Uchida wanted to see Japanese "of some means and education come to Florida and engage in farming of their own account," and he asked that Floridians help make them responsible contributors to American society.

Raising the topic of Japan's progress toward victory in the Russo-Japanese War, Uchida conveyed his gratitude for America's support during the conflict. The atmosphere of the banquet was decidedly sympathetic toward the Japanese cause, with Americans once again expressing approval of a Japanese victory over the Russians.

Discord and Separation

The colony's tomato crop turned out well, and the first weeks of the colony project passed without further dissension. The *Japanese-American Commercial Weekly*, a Japanese-language newspaper published in New York, described conditions in the colony this way in an article that appeared April 1, 1905:

> Fifteen of our countrymen under the leadership of Mr. Sakai really deserve our admiration for toiling so diligently as sweat pours from their bodies darkly tanned beneath the hot sun. Many of the colonists, including Mr. Sakai, are well-educated and no strangers to reading and writing, while among them are certain individuals who bring with them special talents. We think they are highly representative of the Japanese race and have earned the admiration of those who live close by and know them well. Mr. Sakai says that, while they are currently raising tomatoes, from next year he promises to introduce rice production, sericulture, and pineapple cultivation.

This was not to say that no other problems arose, however. Trouble occurred when the time came to ship the colonists' tomato harvest to markets in the North. The shipping company that the settlers were to use by terms of their contract with Ingraham was dissatisfied with the packing tent and packing method the Japanese employed. The company then humiliated and exasperated the settlers with overbearing orders to make improvements. Sakai and the others protested to Ingraham. Since they were under contract with this company, though, they could do nothing but obey. Despite everything, complying with the company contract was the most reasonable and economic option available to them, at least for the time being.

Discontented with the outcome of this conflict, Sakai informed the Model Land Company that he wanted to investigate undeveloped land available for agriculture south of Miami. This news, along with the common occurrence of outsiders approaching Sakai's group to sell them property away from Boca Raton, seemed to put the colony project in jeopardy. If Sakai's group relocated to another site, then the Model Land Company's investment and assistance would be wasted. Fearing this outcome, Ingraham tried to persuade Sakai to give up the idea of relocating, claiming that the land south of Miami was too far from other settlements and unsuitable for farming. He also warned outside instigators to keep away from Sakai and his colonists.

The greatest problem arose among the Japanese themselves. A group of colonists separating from the others and stating that they wanted to be independent rebelled against Sakai's leadership. Six colony members, including Nobuji Inouye, complaining bitterly about Sakai, signed a letter to Rickards, who was overseeing the colony's welfare:

> We told you [the] other day about Sakai's trouble [that is, our trouble with Sakai] as you know we had [a] meeting [with you] when we got [a] good time to [be] independent [from] him. . . . We can not work under such uncivilized people: [although we] do not like to talk about trouble that is [a] very dirty shame between our peoples. We think you do not like to hear such trouble from us, but it could not [be helped, so] please allow me.
>
> We must tell you about trouble between Sakai and us since we arrived [in] Boca Ratone. [Before] we arrived here we . . . believed him very much, so we [left] our native land which is very far from here you know, and we had good hope to commence our new settlement. By and [b]y his treatment [became] very cruel, so we found [we] can not believe him at all. . . . As we said [we] can not work with him at all. I do not know what we shall do, either. . . . Please answer your opinion. . . . We [harvested a] pretty good [crop of] tomato[es] 2,600 plant[s], [so] we can pay off [our] RR Co. debt.

Since no written record exists of the precise reason for the defection from Sakai's leadership, it remains a mystery. Certainly the unexpected state of affairs baffled both Rickards and Ingraham. Since the contract with Sakai committed them to the support of a single colony with Sakai as the sole leader, they took the position that division of the colony in two was unacceptable. Rickards at once assumed the role of intermediary, explaining the company's policy to the "rebels" in an attempt to reunite them with Sakai's group.

Since division of the colony was not a viable option, Inouye and several others of his group soon left. While this problem was resolving itself, the remaining Japanese got the horse and wagon they had wanted so badly. The young men were happy to have the horse to help them work in the field and haul supplies and the crops that they harvested.

"Florida's Yamato Village"

As the colony defectors aired their grievances, Sakai continued to negotiate with the Model Land Company concerning a permanent site for the colony, which had been farming Rickards's land on a temporary basis. As a result, a tract of land between Boca Raton and its neighbor to the north, Delray Beach, became the principal candidate for the new location. Named Wyman, the area was already the location of a pineapple farm called the Keystone Plantation.

Wanting to sell off some of the Keystone Plantation land, the farm's manager initially approached Sakai with an offer. The Model Land Company wanted the colony to buy property that the railroad subsidiary owned, and it naturally objected to Sakai making a deal with the Keystone Plantation. Because the Model Land Company owned acreage adjacent to the plantation, it purchased some of the plantation land, and, combining it with its own property, reserved a tract amounting to 140 acres for Sakai and his group.

In this way a settlement was finally reached between Sakai, the Model Land Company, and the Keystone Plantation. In July 1905, the Yamato Colony, a village made up of Japanese settlers, was established at Wyman, which otherwise had little to boast of but a small post office. In its issue for July 22, 1905, the *Japanese-American Commercial Weekly* in New York reported on the establishment of the colony in detail in an article titled, "Florida's Yamato Village." Rather than a colony, the paper called the settlement a village (*mura*), since among themselves the settlers referred to it as such.

Florida's Yamato Village
Under the leadership of Mr. Jo Sakai since last year, [a colony enterprise] is being operated by approximately twenty individuals in Boca Raton, Florida. Crops have consisted chiefly of tomatoes, cucumbers, etc., with which, they said, they have had good results, bringing in more than $4,000. Within the next year, they will move to a location in Florida called Wyman, and have already signed a contract to purchase a 1,100-acre tract of land there. At present they are in the middle of preparing to move to the new site. Recently, Mr. Sakai, the manager, paid a visit to New York to investigate markets for selling [the colony's] produce and to buy farming implements and equipment. In the near future, Mr. Miyachi, who is one of the members of the association, will return to Japan in order to move forward on their Japanese immigration plan [to bring settlers from Japan]. The Wyman tract, to which they must relocate, is better than the colony's existing location because of its good soil and the convenient shipping it affords. Fruit that the [association members] will grow are apricots, watermelons, melons, etc., while vegetables are chiefly tomatoes along with cucumbers, eggplants, and string beans, among others. Also, they will obtain from Japan seeds for crops not already grown in Florida, which will greatly expand the kinds of crops they produce. The Wyman area from now on is to be named Yamato Village as it is a pioneering settlement of Japanese immigrants to be established permanently. Our fellow countrymen who are presently at Yamato Village are university graduates and graduates of higher middle school and business school, while perhaps only two of them are genuine farmers. We ought to truly congratulate the commencement of a permanent undertaking such as this by our fellow countrymen.

At the end of the Russo-Japanese War, Japanese foreign minister Jutarō Komura, entrusted with full powers to negotiate a peace settlement with Russia, traveled to Portsmouth, New Hampshire, to meet with his Russian counterparts. The SS *Minnesota* carried the foreign minister and his party across the Pacific and docked in Seattle. Japanese negotiators then traveled by rail to Chicago and New York. There, in a pre-negotiations meeting that included Consul General Uchida, Komura's party conferred with President Theodore Roosevelt, who would serve as mediator to the peace talks.

Reclaiming Swampland Inhabited by Snakes and Alligators

On July 31, 1905, as the Japanese in New York prepared for peace talks with the Russians, the *Miami Metropolis* newspaper carried a public-relations supplement from the Florida East Coast Railway that featured a story from Key West. In it, Flagler formally announced plans to extend the railroad tracks, which had been laid as far as Miami, across the sea to Key West.

Flagler's plan called for linking together the dozens of large and small islands of the Florida Keys with bridges erected between them and tracks laid over these bridges from one island to the next. From Miami to Key West the tracks would extend for a total of 150 miles, with about half of the total distance over either swampland or open water. This was the grand, even audacious, plan for extending the railroad that Flagler launched formally.

Flagler, who was struggling with the engineering marvel that would become the Overseas Railroad, was pleased when news of a Japanese colony being established in southern Florida reached his ear. The Japanese colonists did not always fully understand what was going on around them, but they were aware of Flagler's plan to extend the railroad. As they followed his advances they worked hard to clear their fields and get them ready for planting.

Many of the colonists, who were almost all intellectuals and men of means without prior farming experience, did not understand the nature of the work they were to do. Although the process of clearing the subtropical landscape was not complicated, it was physically demanding to a degree that the Japanese did not anticipate. As early summer approached, the increasing heat and humidity made their task that much more difficult. The colony was situated at 26° north latitude, about the

Yamato Station on the Florida East Coast Railway, ca. 1910 (courtesy Morikami Museum and Japanese Gardens).

same as Naha, Japan's southernmost major city. Southern Florida has a subtropical climate, and between May and October its average high temperature exceeds 85° F. At the height of summer, torrential rainfall occurs and mosquitoes attack in swarms, while the temperature climbs to over 90°, which can seem like 100° as a result of the high humidity. As they worked in their fields, the farmers normally wore netting over their heads as protection against the mosquitoes and gnats. Working in such conditions, the Yamato colonists cut back and removed palmettoes and pine trees and prepared their fields for their crops.

Using hoes, rakes, and other tools, the settlers worked by hand without the benefit of machines, advancing a little at a time. Because so much of the property was swampy, they had to plan for drainage as well. Despite the countermeasures they put into place against flooding, when rain fell hard enough their fields sometimes became submerged, ruining their crops.

The colonists also encountered poisonous snakes and alligators, so they carried shotguns for protection. What is more, armed robbers sometimes showed up, intent on stealing from them. They returned fire when the robbers shot at them, but such instances were not like shootouts seen in movie Westerns. Instead, the Japanese settlers found them to be deeply upsetting experiences.

Still, with the cooperation of others who lived nearby like Frank Chesebro, the colonists cleared their land a little at a time and built simple cabins of pine lumber. As the colony's development proceeded in this manner, a milestone event at the colony site took place in 1906, one year after the settlers moved to Wyman. The Florida East Coast Railway constructed a new train station adjacent to the railroad track near the colonists' houses and fields.

In America, where new communities were carved out of the wilderness, the practice of naming them after pioneer settlers was commonplace. Since the Japanese colonists in Florida had named their settlement Yamato, that became the name of the new train station as well.

The station building was a simple structure beside a platform that was only a little higher than the railroad tracks. It was mostly open to the elements, not much more than a roof supported by slender posts. But attached securely above the eaves was a narrow signboard with the name "YAMATO" written across it. Nearby, also adjacent to the railroad track, was a packinghouse for the efficient packing and shipping of

Yamato colonists gathered at the railroad siding, ca. 1911 (courtesy Morikami Museum and Japanese Gardens).

vegetables, pineapples, and other produce to markets in the Northeast and Midwest.

Sakai could only create the community, or village, of Yamato if the colony of Yamato consisted of enough Japanese individuals. In order to achieve this goal, the colony founder tried recruiting families in Japan. Unable to attract significant numbers of them, he instead recruited young single men. Not all of them worked out. Settlers like Inouye who were not destined to last in southern Florida quickly showed their true selves. Yet recruits from the area of Sakai's hometown of Miyazu, or who were members of his extended family, now and then left Japan to join his colony effort. In so doing, they allowed Sakai to accomplish his vision of a village of Japanese.

Hoping to maintain a bond of community among the colonists, Sakai called for the formation of a Yamato Colony Association. In a formal document, he laid out articles of incorporation for the new organization. "The object of this association," he wrote, "shall be to encourage and develop the spirit of colonization among our people of Japan toward the United States; to build up our ideal colony and to inculcate the highest principles and honor as a Japanese colony; to study and improve local farm work; and to introduce Japanese industries which we can adapt to the place and which may tend to advance the industries of Florida and to secure mutual benefits."

The articles further state, "The association is incorporated by the Japanese and the members must be of the Japanese nation." Additional provisions read as follows:

> Any Japanese who settles permanently on Yamato or its suburbs may become a member of this association by signing the contracts and agreeing to be governed by the constitution and rules of the association upon payment of the initiation fee.
>
> . . . The officers of the association shall consist of a manager, a secretary and a treasurer.
>
> The officers of the association as authorized by this constitution, shall be elected by ballot at the annual meeting to be held in October.
>
> . . . To create a fund for the association, all members thereof shall assist in clearing two acres of pine lands, and in planting and

cultivating pineapples on the same during the year. . . . The general and special expenses of the association shall be paid by the produce from the pineapple farm.

A violation of the constitution, or of the by-laws, and any act or acts contrary to the spirit of a true Japanese; and any act of damage to the association, or any member of the association, shall be [punishable by] expulsion from membership in the association.

Embodied in this document were the hopes and dreams of Sakai's colony.

George Morikami Makes His Way to Yamato

In 1906, a number of new colonists made the journey from Japan, among them George Morikami. Traveling for forty-eight days after leaving Yokohama, Morikami arrived at the Yamato Colony on May 15. Although Japanese-American relations in 1906 were worsening where immigration was concerned, Japanese coming to the US continued to enter the country uninterrupted. Landing in Seattle or San Francisco, they spread throughout the West Coast states and to all other parts of the United States as well.

Morikami's ocean voyage seemed to be endless, his train ride across the country long and uncomfortable. Unaccustomed to the only food available, he grew thinner by the day as he journeyed to Florida. When he got off the train, a wagon waited for him at the station. It jolted back and forth over a road that passed through what seemed to be a jungle until at long last it arrived at the village where his fellow countrymen lived and worked. The time was 9:00 p.m.

When Morikami arrived, much of the fields had already been cleared. In the sandy soil pineapple plants with their sharp, spiny leaves spread out in row after row like waves. Pine trees stood at the edges of the fields with needle-laden branches clustered at their tops. Morikami's living accommodations were in a tent or a crudely constructed wood shack. Because Yamato was located close to the ocean, scrap lumber from an old shipwreck had been used in building the shack.

Morikami immediately began working in the fields with Sakai and the others. As it was early summer, the heat and humidity were already quite unbearable. The thick clouds of large mosquitoes, which emitted a whining sound when flying, caused Morikami to exclaim in astonishment, "Why, they're just like dragonflies!" Gnats also swarmed about him. While wearing a net to keep bugs from getting into his mouth and eyes and enduring the heat, he plowed, then planted pineapple plants.

Unaccustomed to such strenuous work, Morikami spent his first New Year's in Florida sick with a fever. He had also lost weight. To stave off hunger he drank powdered milk and ate crackers.

Newspapers published in Florida at the time showed an interest in the daily lives of the newcomers from Japan, and occasionally carried stories about them. An October 13, 1906, artcle in the *Tropical Sun*, a newspaper published in West Palm Beach, thirty-five miles north of the colony, was the first to introduce "Yamato" to English speakers as the name of the Japanese colony.

At the same time, the name of the small Wyman post office, which was near the Yamato Colony site, was also changed to Yamato. The residents of this area were almost all Yamato colonists. Sakai appealed to postal authorities to make the change, in order to conform with the name of the newly established train station. In addition, mail was stamped with a Yamato postmark. An elementary school also sharing the name was built once married men in the colony increased in number and started families.

Soon after arriving in southern Florida, as the colonists became accustomed to their new surroundings, they received an invitation to the Dade County Fair in March 1905. In July, they took part in the celebration of the city of Miami's tenth anniversary. Their attendance at both of these events was noted in the press. Around Thanksgiving Day, 1907, Sakai took the initiative to invite Model Land Company president James Ingraham and his wife to visit Yamato. Sakai and his wife personally greeted Mr. and Mrs. Ingraham at the Yamato train station and showed them around during their visit. To their delight, the Ingrahams found the Sakai house decorated to create an East Asian atmosphere.

The *Daily Miami Metropolis* provided its readers with details:

Blood red beets carved to represent magnificent roses formed an artistic combination with roses carved from white turnips. The deception was very clever and the effect all that could be desired. . . .

After dinner an exhibition of jiu-jitsu, Japanese fencing and wrestling entertained the guests. The latter were escorted to the town hall where eighteen stalwart Japs were arranged for the contest. . . . Their exhibition was realistic in the extreme, especially the fencing bouts. They were dressed in suits of armor . . . and used bamboo swords. Points are counted for touching the head, neck or wrist, as in actual combat these would be disabling thrusts or blows. The fencing armor and other equipment was brought over by Sakai on the last visit to Japan.

For quite a while wrestling and jiu-jitsu entertained Mr. Ingraham and family and then the Japanese gave interpretations of a Japanese war song, all the participants being in the orthodox costume of their country used for such occasions. The program . . . was followed by music on Japanese instruments. One of the Japanese women favored the visitors with a song, accompanying herself on [two] Japanese stringed instruments. The notes of these instruments were somewhat weird, but not harsh or discordant like the Chinese music.

Because it was located midway between Boca Raton and Delray Beach (called simply Delray at the time), the Yamato colonists also participated as a village in Delray Beach's celebrations. For Independence

Delray Independence Day parade, 1914, featuring two horse-drawn floats from Yamato, one displaying a giant tomato (courtesy Delray Beach Historical Society).

Day they constructed their own floats and entered them in the parade that took place on the town's main street. In 1913, one float consisted of a large replica of a tomato, the colonists' most important crop, placed on a wagon drawn by a single horse. Another float, a wagon pulled by a pair of horses, featured a *torii*, or emblematic gateway of a Shintō shrine. The wagon was decorated on all sides with flowers and star-spangled red-white-and-blue bunting. Men from Yamato rode on both wagons, the drivers handling the reins with pride.

A Fortune from Silk Crepe and the Death of Mitsusaburo Oki

In December 1906, the colonists experienced an event that had not oc-curred since Yamato's inception. Mitsusaburo Oki, who had been the chief financier of Sakai's enterprise and the oldest member of the col-ony, passed away. At that time typhoid fever had grown to an epidemic, spreading everywhere. In many communities in southern Florida, Americans died in large numbers, and even some colonists succumbed to the disease. Typhoid fever was believed to have been the cause of Oki's death as well.

Oki, the brother-in-law of Jo Sakai, had invested a considerable sum of money in developing the colony. He had sufficient funds available to him to act as his own bank. Oki amassed his wealth as co-owner of a wholesale silk business, Oki Shōten. Businesses related to the raw silk and silk crepe (*chirimen*) industries were lined side by side on the main street of Oki's hometown of Mineyama, located in the middle of the Tango Peninsula. In front of these shops hung signboards bearing such legends as "Silk-Thread Spinning," "Chirimen Brokerage Company," "Silk Crepe—All Varieties, Manufacture and Sales," and "Silkworm Egg-Cards Available Here."

Chirimen is a fabric in which the horizontal, or weft, threads are given a strong twist in the weaving process while the vertical, or warp, threads are not. This twisting of the threads imparts a distinctive wavy or crimped texture to the fabric, called *shibo* (grain), which emerges suddenly after the refining process.

The Tango area has long been a center for the production of silk tex-tiles. In 1720, Saheiji Kinuya of Mineyama introduced the techniques of creating chirimen silk crepe from the Kyōto weaving district of Nishijin, and since then the weaving industry has prospered everywhere on the Tango Peninsula. By the end of the nineteenth century, even common people took to wearing silk *kimonos*—for example, formal wear for making house calls or the long-sleeved garments called *furisode* favored by young women—thus increasing the demand for silk crepe.

After the Seinan War of 1877, Tango experienced an economic boom in which the wholesale silk crepe business prospered. Although hard times followed, the chirimen industry was on a firm footing once again by the end of the Russo-Japanese War when Oki accompanied Sakai to Florida.

A chirimen wholesale district became established in Mineyama around 1890. The area had not only businesses in the Tango chirimen trade, handsomely appointed with tiled roofs and windows featuring finely spaced lattices, but also restaurants, inns, dry-goods stores, pharmacies, lumber dealers, and bicycle shops. By 1900, leading silk dealers in Mineyama had also set up branches in Muromachi, the center of Kyōto's mercantile district. Among them was Oki Shōten, the wholesale business run by Risaburo and Mitsusaburo Oki.

At the same time Kyōto's wholesale textile dealers also established themselves in Mineyama. Traffic between the Tango Peninsula and Kyōto was brisk. Merchants coming to Mineyama to buy silk crepe, including representatives of such silk manufacturers as Fujibō, Kanebō, and Katakura, all major corporations today, traded with Oki Shōten. On most evenings the Oki brothers hosted receptions at one of the local restaurants where they warmly welcomed clients and discussed business over drinks. Employing as many as sixty or seventy *geisha* on a typical evening, their success seemed to be such that, if they wanted, they could hire every *geisha* in town.

Raw silk, from which chirimen was made, was Japan's leading export commodity, with exports valued at ¥6.65 million (approximately 40 percent of total exports) in 1868 and ¥19.14 million in 1882 (approximately 50 percent of total exports). What is more, during the two years of the Sino-Japanese War, 1894 and 1895, this figure swelled to nearly ¥87 million. Considering that the total expenditure for prosecuting the war against China was ¥200 million, ¥87 million was quite a substantial income.

Exports declined somewhat in 1904 during the Russo-Japanese War, but once victory was achieved the following year, they recovered rapidly. Exports of raw silk in 1906 surpassed a total of ¥100 million. Trading companies like Mitsui had already set up branch offices in New York in order to export raw silk directly to American clients, while in Yokohama an exchange was established for what were termed the "Four Commodities." The Four Commodities were silk yarn (which actually was not handled through the exchange), processed tea, textiles, and marine products.

Since raw silk, which fell under the rubric of textiles, dominated trade at the exchange, it was commonly called the Raw Silk Exchange. Because of the exchange, the price of raw silk became public knowledge, allowing a market price to be established. At the same time, any changes affecting the outlook of raw silk as a commodity prompted speculation that in turn caused the market price to become volatile.

Some dealers in the silk trade bought raw silk, had it woven in the domestic cottage weaving industry, and sold it wholesale. But as silk prices rose, many in the trade no longer found dealing on such a small scale profitable.

For silk dealers to determine the market price of raw silk even locally, it was necessary for them to take the international situation into consideration. Thus Oki Shōten and the other principal silk merchants of Mineyama kept a close eye on world trends. If silk prices were predicted to rise, merchants profited from increasing their purchases, but they also stood to double their profits by buying on credit. Those who observed the normal ups and downs of the silk market were often tempted to manipulate it, some doing so successfully, others failing bitterly. While chirimen itself was a commodity admired for its beauty, in truth the silk trade business had a dark side in market speculation of this kind.

The Okis were among the merchants of Mineyama who marketed chirimen textiles overseas in Asia and elsewhere. As entrepreneurs they traveled extensively to Taiwan, the Philippines, Shanghai, Macao, Hong Kong, and Sydney, Australia, in search of markets for their wares. Later, they met with success in the United States as well.

In the Tango area, the local community benefited indirectly from the chirimen industry. For example, Isuke Yoshimura of Yoshimura Shōten, established a bank in Mineyama with his fortune in earnings from Tango chirimen. Besides being a leader in the chirimen industry and becoming mayor of the town, he contributed his own money toward the construction of Mineyama's public waterworks. Furthermore, he established a not-for-profit foundation dedicated to nurturing young talent in the community. He became involved in providing scholarships to students as a result. Yoshimura also was elected as a representative to the Diet, Japan's national parliament, thus contributing both publicly and privately to the benefit of the region. This, too, was evidence of the financial power provided by the Tango chirimen industry.

As for the Oki brothers, they chose to invest in America. Flagler made a fortune in the oil business during the Gilded Age and contributed his wealth in part to the development of Florida. So too was the wealth created in far-off Japan through the chirimen silk industry invested in the state.

Mitsusaburo Oki had traveled to the United States aboard the SS *Manchuria* from Kōbe to San Francisco. After living in Florida for two years, he passed away at forty-nine years of age without seeing the final result of his work. A Christian funeral service was held for him according to family wishes, and his body was cremated. About twenty Japanese from the colony attended the funeral, their stoic demeanor making a strong impression on the Americans who were present as well.

Oki's death gave the colonists a jolt. George Morikami, for one, did not know what to expect from this development. If Morikami completed the three-year period of his contract, would he satisfy his responsibility to the colony project? More to the point, would he receive the $500 bonus? Looking at the earnings of immigrants at the time, it was a substantial sum of money equal to a full year's pay for work as a railroad construction worker or a farm laborer. Returning home with this money and using it to buy land and plant an orchard was the dream that Morikami had had from the beginning.

Now that Oki had passed away, Morikami was uncertain whether he would receive the $500 if he worked as promised. Without a penny to his name, he could do nothing but continue to work despite his feelings of anxiety. On the other hand, when Oki's family in Mineyama received word that he had died, they could not understand how his death could have happened, and they felt that Florida must be a terrible place.

Squeezed by Pineapples from Cuba

The death of Mitsusaburo Oki did nothing to change the colony's organization or its goals. It continued as before, the colony members making satisfactory progress in cultivating pineapples and winter vegetables. On January 18, 1908, Sakai reported on the colony's success in an article titled "Dispatch from Florida" appearing in the *Japanese-American Commercial Weekly*:

Dispatch from Florida
This year prospects at Yamato Village are greatly improved. Our success is such that we have not seen before. Regarding our progress, the first point is that until last year we were renting our vegetable fields, but from the current year we will purchase more than five acres of land per person. More importantly, we have found land that is better than that of our neighbors. At present we are preparing to plant our crops, and planting them. Without a doubt we will ship more than 20,000 crates of tomatoes this year, even if they are picked only by the Japanese men of Yamato, and expect to bring in earnings of over $40,000.

When Consul General Koike and Mr. Hatsumi Ōkura come to Florida, they will be happy to see that the colony members have been blessed with tremendous gains and are much satisfied. Many will surely discover that, having inspected this location, we certainly surpass any other colony without fail. Actually, even someone like Tatsuyuki Nakajima, whose younger brother will begin farming operations in Texas, recognizes that this area's future prospects are exceedingly good. Mr. Nakajima has sent a telegram to his younger brother to invite him to come and compare Florida and Texas to judge for himself whether our operation has a future here. Although farming is extremely easy, it does require attention and experience, and will not succeed based solely on the size of one's investment.

Shown below is a chart of the acreage devoted to pineapples and estimated yields for the present year:

Tsujii Group	6 acres	1,500 crates
Murakami Group	1 acre	250 crates

Sakai Group	4 acres	1,400 crates
Kamiya Group	⅓ acre	100 crates
Yoshida Group	1½ acres	450 crates
Okudaira Group	13 acres	1,500 crates
Oki-Sakai Cooperative	17 acres	5,000 crates

In his *Commercial Weekly* article, Sakai told his readers that the colonists were having success raising tomatoes and hoped to enlarge their land-holdings. Furthermore, he tried to persuade readers that to visit Florida was to see for themselves that the state held out greater promise than did Texas.

Sakai's article also showed how the Yamato Colony was organized, with the colonists divided into separate groups, each of which brought in a part of the total colony harvest. Some of the Yamato land was owned cooperatively, but some land was owned individually by settlers who managed it under their own names rather than that of the colony.

A local journal devoted to Florida agriculture, the *Florida Farmer's Homeseeker* (also known as the *Florida East Coast Homeseeker*) also carried an occasional article on what was happening in the colony. The following appeared in the July 1908 issue:

> The Japanese growers at Yamato are thriving. Last week two [train] cars of pine[apple]s were exported to England. One grower shipped 800 crates of tomatoes, which netted him $2 a crate.
>
> J. Sakai and T. Ishibashi, from Yamato, came to [West Palm Beach] this morning on bicycles to transact business at the local stores. They report having shipped eight cars of pineapples and will have five cars more. They say that their tomato crop did not pan out very well, but the pineapple crop is quite satisfactory, considering the weather conditions of this year.

In the November issue the same journal reported that the results of the farming efforts at Yamato were becoming increasingly successful:

> It was [at Yamato] that sixteen men, under the leadership of J. Sakai, came in 1904 and settled on 140 acres of land, where they immediately began clearing. They have now about seventy acres in pineapples, and last year they had a hundred acres in vegetables, and they have purchased more land individually.

Their lands are splendidly adapted to the growing of the pineapple, and their fields are handsome as any to be found on the East Coast.... There is not a lazy bone in the body of these people, and they have a way of working that makes every effort count, and that the colony will be a success is without question.

There are some forty people in the settlement at this time, among them being two women. Mr. Sakai, the manager of the colony, went to Japan last year, and when he returned he brought with him a wife. Mr. Sakai has an interest in twenty-five acres in pineapples, and this year is planning to set out a large quantity of grapefruit and other citrus trees.

A leading man in the colony is Count Okudaira, a member of the royal household of Japan. He has twenty-seven acres in pineapples and is interested in the vegetable fields of Yamato.

Yet another issue of the *Homeseeker* stated that in 1908 the southeastern coast of Florida where Yamato was located was not affected by the recession suffered in most other parts of the country. Area farmers were able to ship large quantities of fruits and vegetables to markets in the North. The region, which had the largest percentage of pineapples under cultivation anywhere in the state, was developing rapidly, while progress showed every sign of continuing in the following year.

However, after predictions of this kind appeared in print, pineapple crops suffered from blight caused by nematodes and production fell sharply. Furthermore, Florida growers were sidelined in the marketplace by less expensive pineapples grown in Cuba. When Cuban pineapples came into the picture, prices declined by as much as a third of what they had been previously. Dissatisfaction among local farmers had been building since 1903, and a movement arose to demand government protection. Unable to compete with its Cuban competition, the Florida pineapple industry was on the verge of collapse.

At Yamato, pineapples accounted for more than half of the colony's total output. In the face of Cuban competition, the colonists decided to simply switch their winter crop from pineapples to winter vegetables. The transition occurred smoothly. The colony's vegetables earned high praise, and the colonists increased their yield per acre.

The Japanese of Florida

Escorting Brides from Japan

The original members of the Yamato Colony traveled without spouses to the United States, but several of them later brought wives from Japan. The first to do so was Jo Sakai, who married Sada Kawashima in 1907 during a visit to Japan. Sada was born into a former *samurai* household from Zeze, Shiga Prefecture. At the age of nineteen she joined the Yamato Colony as its first known woman inhabitant.

In order to encourage Yamato's growth as a community, Sakai hoped that Sada would support his role by assuming a leadership position among the women of the colony as they arrived. But Sada, who was an introvert by nature, never felt comfortable in such a role. When she arrived in Florida and saw Yamato for the first time, she was disappointed that it was not more developed. Yet as the need arose, she could hold her own while bargaining with local Native Americans for such things as furs and corn.

Toward the end of her first year in Florida, Sada gave birth to a son. The couple named the child Hiroshi, but he died at just shy of sixteen months of age. Following a period of grief, a daughter, Chikako Katherine Sakai, was born. Chikako was followed by four more daughters, the youngest, whom they named Itsuko, born in 1918.

Two years after the marriage of Jo and Sada Sakai, Jo's younger brother Tamemasu (Henry) Kamiya also returned to the brothers' hometown of Miyazu and married elementary school teacher Yetsu Oishi, whom he brought to Yamato. The Kamiyas had six children, three boys and three girls. In 1915, Jinzo Yamauchi, who was from Oki's hometown of Mineyama (today Kyōtango City), returned to Japan to marry Naka Bamba, the daughter of another *chirimen* wholesale dealer. The Yamauchis also raised a family at Yamato.

Hideo Kobayashi was born into the household of a large landowner in Japan. He grew up in Oku-Takeno, a secluded village in Kinosaki District, Hyōgo Prefecture (today part of Toyooka City), which lay along the upper reaches of the Takeno River six miles or so inland from the Japan Sea. Although he was a farmer, Kobayashi's father, Tōsuke, served on the Oku-Takeno village council and as village headman after serving as a member of the Hyōgo Prefectural Assembly.

Born in 1883, Hideo was the fourth son born into the Kobayashi family. He was persuaded to come to the United States by a relative, Aisuke Tsujii, who came from the Tango Peninsula and was a member of the Yamato Colony in its early days. Kobayashi arrived in Florida in 1907, a year following Morikami. Twelve years later he returned to his hometown to marry. His bride was Umeko Kono, from Matsuyama, Aichi Prefecture. The first time they set eyes on one another was at their wedding ceremony. Soon after their marriage, Kobayashi brought Umeko to Florida, where they began raising a family. The year after Umeko's arrival, the couple's first child, Theodore Sakaye Kobayashi, was born.

Susumu Kobayashi, who joined the colony much later, hailed from the town of Hirata (today part of Izumo City) in Shimane Prefecture. Kobayashi was the second son of a physician in a long line of physicians. After graduating from middle school, he attended the predecessor of Ritsumeikan University in Kyōto. Not long afterward, his sister married a man named Kawashima, who owned a Kyōto antique store and was the elder brother of Sada Sakai, wife of Yamato Colony founder Jo Sakai. Because of his relation through marriage to the Sakais, he decided to join the colony effort in America. In 1914, at the age of twenty-two, he landed in the US at Seattle and, after spending a night in Chicago, made his way to Yamato. In order to distinguish himself from

Hideo Kobayashi, who was already a colony member, he adopted the name Oscar.

After the Gentlemen's Agreement halted immigration of Japanese laborers to the United States, the manner of bringing wives from Japan as "picture brides" became widespread. Couples exchanged photographs, and on that basis alone, they decided whether to marry before ever meeting their prospective spouses. Afterward the "brides" would travel across the Pacific unaccompanied to meet their husbands for the first time on the docks of San Francisco or Seattle. In American society, the practice was criticized as callous, even inhumane. Many of the Yamato men—Hideo Kobayashi, for example—were sensitive to this attitude. They returned to Japan to meet future partners, then marry and escort their brides to Florida. It was a courtesy that they could afford, unlike many other Japanese immigrant men.

Even as wives joined the colony, however, others gave up on it and left. One reason may have been that the once-rosy future of the pineapple as a viable commercial crop began to look doubtful. Others who made the decision to leave did so because of the risk of contracting malaria, or because they could not endure Florida's summertime heat and humidity.

Akira Hada Ohnishi, who came to the US after graduating from Dōshisha's English language school, settled in the colony with his wife of European ancestry, Iola. She gave birth to the first child born in the colony but succumbed to illness and died in 1907. Her husband elected not to remain at Yamato. A settler named Tahara and his French-born wife also settled in the colony for a time, but like Ohnishi they, too, left before long.

Masakuni Okudaira, who farmed his own land in the colony and was one of its early leaders, also went to New York when necessary to purchase supplies and conduct other business. His elder brother Count Masayasu Okudaira was a member of the House of Peers and head of the Okudaira family. Masayasu, who had also studied abroad as both his father and his younger brother had done, strongly urged Masakuni to give up farming in Florida and return to Japan. Heeding his brother's advice, Masakuni, too, soon departed from Yamato.

Among other colonists were those whom Sakai had recruited in New York and elsewhere in the United States, and a few who had come

Gathering of Yamato families, ca. 1922 (courtesy Morikami Museum and Japanese Gardens).

to join family members who were already colony members. Some colonists had joined after hearing secondhand about Sakai's plans for Yamato.

Shikazo Ashida was from Higashi Asahikawa, Kamikawa District (today part of Asahikawa City), on Hokkaidō, Japan's northernmost main island. He traveled to the US in 1903 but was drafted into the Japanese Imperial Army the following year with the outbreak of the war with Russia. For his military service Ashida was awarded the Order of the Sacred Treasure, sixth class. He married in 1906 and again traveled to the United States. After spending time in California, he and his wife, Shizuyo, went to Yamato in 1914, bought farmland, and settled down.

Gengoro (George or G. G.) Yoshida, from Morioka, Iwate Prefecture, traveled to the US in 1907. The following year he went to Florida, but he did not join the colony effort at Yamato for several years. Afterward, he married Katsu (Jean) Narita, who was from Hirosaki, Aomori Prefecture. Her family had already relocated to upstate New York by the time the couple met. They started a family while living at Yamato.

Shohbi Kamikama, who was from the Satsuma Peninsula in Kagoshima Prefecture in southwestern Japan, ventured to America in 1907. Arriving in Seattle, Kamikama went to New York, where he worked as a waiter. In 1917, after catching a vicious cold, he decided he could no longer endure New York's cold winters and went to Yamato.

In 1908, the *Florida Farmer's Homeseeker* put Yamato's population at forty settlers occupying 140 acres of land. By 1910, the colony had dwindled to fewer than thirty individuals. Japanese immigration figures show a similar trend nationally for the early twentieth century. Between 1909 and 1910, 8,500 Japanese immigrants came to the United States. In comparison, 15,000 individuals, or nearly twice the number of arrivals, returned to Japan over the same period.

A Life of Their Own Making between East and West

For the Yamato colonists, the physical environment of Florida was unlike anything they had encountered in Japan. They experienced hurricanes strong enough to blow over a house, frequently heavy downpours, and lightning strikes. Just when the settlers thought that that was all they could expect, days of stifling heat followed one after another with no rainfall in sight.

In winter, frosts occurred. When frost was in the forecast, farmers took such safeguards as covering crops with yards of a fabric similar to cheesecloth, according to Sumiko Kobayashi, daughter of Yamato settlers Oscar and Suye Kobayashi. Such precautions, of course, did not protect against damage from heavy rainfall. Usually farmers in Florida began shipping their produce to markets in the North around Thanksgiving Day. In those years when rain devastated crops, the fields had to be replanted. Only with difficulty were farmers able to ship produce by January at the earliest, writes Kobayashi in a monograph titled "Yamato, Florida: A Japanese Farming Village between Palm Beach and the Everglades."*

Luckily, water was not a problem, since settlers could reach it by digging wells only about fifteen feet or so in depth. The water acquired in this way could be used without further treatment because it was naturally purified as it passed through the limestone bedrock. What is more, such wells were easily dug.

---

* Much of the material in the following sections comes from the unpublished monograph "Yamato, Florida: A Japanese Farming Village between Palm Beach and the Everglades," by Sumiko Kobayashi, who obtained the information through conversations with her mother, Yamato settler Suye Kobayashi.

The greatest obstacle to working outdoors on a farm, however, was the hordes of mosquitoes. In addition, farmworkers were usually tormented by biting flies. The colonists had to wear nets over their heads as protection. At night, mosquitoes collected on the netting in such numbers that one could not see through it.

The settlers had to take care when encountering wildlife such as alligators and poisonous snakes. The men had to be mindful of their surroundings near ditches, canals, and other bodies of water, and they always wore tall protective boots because rattlesnakes were common. George Morikami often snared rabbits, but occasionally he would end up catching a skunk instead. Some of the colonists carried around shotguns in case of emergency. Like cowboys in a movie Western, they rode horseback with their shotguns by their sides. In truth, settlers who appeared to have stepped off a movie screen had unpleasant memories of being attacked by gunmen as they first established the colony. These Yamato residents continued to carry weapons for self-defense.

Working in such unsafe conditions the colonists raised a variety of vegetables, including tomatoes, eggplants, peppers, green beans, lima beans, squash, and other crops, in addition to pineapples. Planting usually began in July. Early harvest ended in September, while the main harvest went on to around Thanksgiving Day. The harvest would continue, though, until May of the following year.

At first mules were used to plow the fields, but later the tractor was introduced for that purpose. Transportation of the crop from the field was also accomplished by mule- or horse-drawn wagon, which by degrees was replaced by the truck. Packing the vegetable crop for shipment took place at the communal packinghouse that had been built beside the railroad tracks. Individual landowners also had their own packing sheds. To get their produce to market, the colonists sometimes contracted with commission agents communally.

After crating, vegetables were loaded onto freight cars chilled with ice, then shipped to New York and other large cities in the Northeast or to Chicago and similar markets in the Midwest. Produce from Yamato went to the Pacific coast as well. The farmers, of course, sought high bids for their produce, but they knew market prices well because prices were regularly wired to them from various cities. Occasionally customers questioned the quality of the produce. On at least one occasion a lawsuit resulted, reveals Sumiko Kobayashi, when rain compromised that quality, and farmers shipped the harvested crops anyway due to customer demand.

When the settlers began clearing the land at the permanent site, they also built houses. This they were able to do because some of them enjoyed a certain financial stability. When he married in 1922, Oscar Kobayashi lived in a single-story house with one bedroom, an L-shaped living room, and a kitchen with storage and a pantry, according to his daughter Sumiko Kobayashi. In the kitchen was a hand pump used to raise water from a well under the house. The Kobayashis bought ice from the general store opened by Henry Kamiya, Jo Sakai's brother. The ice was put into an icebox in which perishable foods were kept fresh. The pantry was regularly stocked with such things as rice, soy sauce, and soybean paste, common items in the Japanese diet.

At night the Kobayashis used kerosene lamps, and around January or February when outdoor temperatures were at their lowest, they warmed themselves using a kerosene heater. When cooking, they used the oven chiefly to bake fish, but women in the different households, including the Kobayashis', also liked to use it to bake biscuits, which were largely unknown in Japan. In addition, the Kobayashis were able to warm bathwater using the heat of the sun. They put water in a couple of tubs and placed them on the back porch in the morning. By evening the sun had more than sufficiently heated the water for bathing. Because there was nothing behind the house but the natural Florida landscape, notes writer Sumiko Kobayashi, the family could bathe in the open without concern.

The two-story Sakai house, next door to the Kobayashi residence, was equipped with electrical appliances powered by a generator. Sada Sakai nevertheless prepared meals using a wood-burning stove. The house also featured a deep Japanese-style bathtub made of wood.

In order to have eggs most households in the colony raised chickens. But settlers purchased bacon, which they ate often, canned goods such as sausage and sardines, and bread and rice at the Kamiya general store. The Kamiya family raised milk cows and hogs. They sold fresh milk to their neighbors and took the hogs to market. In addition to this livestock they owned a mule that they used for work in the fields.

When Oscar Kobayashi once fired his shotgun into a flock of quail that had flown into the yard, he hit a number of the birds with the scattershot. After plucking the quail, the Kobayashis barbecued them in soy sauce and sugar and ate them. The family also liked to eat the large bananas that grew in Florida, unlike any they had seen in Japan, and because fruit trees had been planted between the Kobayashi house and the Sakai house, they had grapefruit and limes as well. With no trouble at all the Kobayashis could catch fresh fish in the ocean, but they also purchased it in Delray Beach.

In her monograph on life in Yamato, Sumiko Kobayashi reports that breakfast at her parents' home was usually American-style, with fruit, toast, bacon and eggs, and coffee. A typical lunch might have consisted of boiled rice with tea poured over it and eggplant or peppers pickled at home. The evening meal was a compromise between East and West. Fish was prepared as uncooked fillets, or *sashimi*, fried as *tempura*, or seasoned with soy sauce or salt and grilled. Meat dishes such as *sukiyaki* made with either chicken or beef and stew with vegetables were prepared at the table. White rice, green tea, and pickled vegetables were usually served as well.

Soy sauce and *miso* (soybean paste) were obtained in barrels or buckets from New York. In the same way, *kakimochi*, or dried sliced rice cakes, had to be obtained from New York as well. The Kobayashis bought canned milk to add to coffee, according to Sumiko Kobayashi, but they rarely used it otherwise in cooking. Jinzo Yamauchi liked to eat rice in an unusual way, with catsup poured over it.

The Kobayashis had an employee do the family's laundry, for which they paid one dollar per washing. Once a week they took their dirty clothes to the employee's house, along with detergent. When the washing was done, Oscar Kobayashi went to pick it up after it had been ironed and folded, according to Sumiko Kobayashi. The Kobayashis asked the employee to launder work clothes, sheets, and underwear. Oscar's wife, Suye, washed her stockings and her baby's diapers herself.

During the time that Oscar Kobayashi lived at Yamato, a loaf of bread cost fifteen cents. A glass of beer and a sandwich purchased at a bar (before Prohibition) was a nickel, notes Sumiko.

In addition to managing his farm, Henry Kamiya opened a general store in Yamato. It carried items useful for everyday life that were purchased not only by the Japanese settlers of the colony but also by their American neighbors. Available at the store besides groceries were shoes, work clothes, and watches. Because colony residents owned automobiles and tractors, the establishment had a couple of gasoline pumps, too. If the Kamiya store did not carry what customers wanted, those customers went to Delray Beach. There, the colonists could see a doctor, obtain medicine, and have their automobiles repaired. They could also order clothing and children's toys by mail using the Sears and Roebuck or Montgomery Ward sales catalogues.

For the very best quality in suits and dresses, the Yamato residents shopped in Palm Beach, Sumiko Kobayashi writes. They might buy several suits at one time, particularly after a successful growing season. Men wore jackets with silk shirts that had removable collars, while women showed off silk dresses. Stylishly dressed in this manner, colonists enjoyed going for rides in their automobiles, which they exchanged for new models almost every year.

Get-Togethers at Jap Rock (Yamato Rock)

In Yamato, Sundays were holidays from work for everyone. Yamato residents enjoyed such activities as swimming and fishing at the nearby beach, but they instead might drive to Palm Beach to see a silent movie and have dinner out at a restaurant. In addition, the men of the colony often gathered at the home of Oscar Kobayashi, where they gambled at cards, including the Japanese game called *hanafuda*, and played pool. Jo Sakai sometimes took the children to see a movie at the theater in Delray Beach. For that matter, he would go with anyone almost anytime to see a movie in West Palm Beach or Miami.

In June, after they finished the harvest but before the next planting began, the colonists went to picnic on the beach almost every day, remarks Sumiko Kobayashi. Low beige dunes lay beside the road along the beach, which the settlers used to drive to the ocean. Beyond the dunes, the bright sand spread to the water's edge and into the azure sea. On days with no breeze, gentle waves rolled in one after another to break on the shore.

On Florida's Atlantic coast, the sandy beach stretches the entire length of the state, from north to south. There are a number of communities in Florida incorporating the word *beach* into their names,

Yamato residents gather under a tent for a get-together at the beach, ca. 1919 (courtesy Sumiko Kobayashi).

communities like Palm Beach and Daytona Beach, where motorcar racing on a twenty-two-mile stretch of oceanfront has taken place since the early twentieth century.

At Delray Beach and Boca Raton, where Yamato was located, the wide beach extended for as far as the eye could see. At the spot on the beach where the Yamato Japanese went for picnics was a rocky outcropping near which they often gathered. Rugged and pitted, the low-lying formation appeared just above the surface of the water. The Japanese preferred this spot, located just across the Intracoastal Waterway from Yamato, where they had erected a shelter to enjoy their picnic meals.

This location could not have been better suited for beach gatherings by the Yamato Japanese, and soon the rocky outcropping had acquired the name Jap Rock among the locals. In Florida, people used the word Jap freely, applying it to the Yamato settlers with no awareness that it was a derogatory term.

The rock was limestone formed from fossilized corals, around which sand had accumulated naturally over the years. It was low enough that at high tide, water would just cover the ankles of a man standing on the formation. In Miyazu and on the Tango Peninsula where Jo Sakai and George Morikami were from, beaches made up much of the seashore. But these locations also featured numerous rocky expanses where the mountain slopes came right down to the water's edge. All it took was a rocky outcropping or two to make a Japanese feel nostalgic for home.

On days when the Yamato settlers had picnics on the beach, they prepared boxed lunches at home before leaving for the beach by car. Once there, fishing was one of their favorite activities. Colonists almost always caught fish like bluefish and snapper, while crabs could be had by the bucketful. Hideo Kobayashi did not use a rod and reel to fish, instead relying only on a fishing line. First he caught small fish, and then he used them as bait to catch fish like snapper, blue runner, and jack. Kobayashi would dry the small fish in the sun on a tin roof. The settlers ate them in salads, Sumiko Kobayashi writes.

While the men were fishing, the women and children collected shells. They used this site on the beach for small get-togethers such as farewell parties. For these gatherings Hideo Kobayashi took pride in making noodles by hand to be used in the soup dish called *udon*. He mixed flour with eggs from the family's hens to make the noodles from scratch, and the Kamiya family provided the stock for the soup from their chickens. Each family contributed pickled vegetables.

Apart from such picnics, some of the men drank when they gathered socially. Beer was not very popular. Yamato's male settlers did drink wine, but what they liked best was bootleg whiskey, according to Sumiko Kobayashi. The women, on the other hand, in what little free time they had between housework and child-rearing, got together to enjoy chatting over tea and cookies or fruit. In the Hideo Kobayashi household, Umeko, Hideo's wife, sometimes hosted simplified Japanese-style ceremonial tea gatherings.

Hideo's family also owned an ice cream–making machine. The children of the neighborhood were delighted whenever Kobayashi treated them to the vanilla ice cream that he made.

For New Year's Day the colonists offered seasonal greetings to one another and got together at the home of either Oscar Kobayashi or Henry Kamiya for a celebration. They made chicken *teriyaki* (morsels of roasted chicken on skewers) and obtained other foods from New York like *kamaboko* (fish paste), *kazunoko* (herring roe), and *kobumaki* (fish rolled in kelp). Foods like these were usually available tinned. The Sakai family ordered *mochi* (rice cakes) from San Francisco, but because of the length of time it took for the cakes to be shipped, mold

Picnics celebrating bountiful harvests (courtesy Morikami Museum and Japanese Gardens).

was often found growing on them once they arrived in Florida, Sumiko Kobayashi reports in her monograph. The settlers had to scrape the rice cakes clean before roasting them to eat.

At Christmas, the colonists followed American custom and exchanged gifts with close friends and family members. On Independence Day everyone went to Delray Beach. Given a little spending money, the children enjoyed the day away from the farm.

After the harvest was over, all of the colonists gathered for an outdoor celebration of a successful year. For their picnic repast, they set up large tables beside a canal. A photograph of such an event suggests that the canal was lined by palm trees. Even in the steamy heat of southern Florida, the men wore either short-sleeved or long-sleeved dress shirts, and some of them also wore neckties. The women favored long-sleeved dresses and wore their hair in a bun in the old-fashioned Japanese *shimada* style. The women changed to styling their hair in Western fashion during the 1920s.

Of course, the Yamato Japanese associated with the wider community as well. Even within the area known as Yamato white families resided, including that of the Yamato postmaster and employees of the Kamiya general store. Japanese children and white children attended school together in a one-room schoolhouse in Yamato. When the school closed, the children continued to attend school in Boca Raton.

Some African American families who worked in the farm fields had lived in the area for many years, but some relative newcomers had moved nearby from various southern states as well as the Bahamas and the Caribbean. The Japanese listened to these residents singing as they worked early in the morning.

The Yamato colonists employed both white and black workers in their farming operations. Whites chiefly handled the packing and

Yamato children attending school at the one-room Yamato schoolhouse with other local children, 1922 (courtesy Morikami Museum and Japanese Gardens).

shipping, while African Americans mostly worked in the fields. Some of the latter individuals were tenant farmers working Japanese-owned land. The Japanese bartered with them for fresh fish, sausage, and other commodities. The colonists also associated with the single Native American living in the area.

Without a family of his own, George Morikami did not often socialize with others in the colony, and he stuck out at community get-togethers like the New Year's celebration. He employed African Americans in his fields, sometimes complaining about their work. Despite this, neither Morikami nor other Yamato colonists discriminated against non-Japanese. Nor were the settlers, in the pre–World War II era at least, victims of discrimination themselves.

Hardly any of the Japanese colonists came to the US as Christians, although some, like Henry Kamiya, were baptized after their arrival. Children in both the Kamiya and Kobayashi families attended Sunday school at a church in Delray Beach.

Another Colony That Failed

The settlers of the Yamato Colony were not the only Japanese living in Florida at the time of the colony's founding. By 1905 or '06 Japanese in Miami had already opened a Japanese art store, while in 1907 or '08, a Japanese opened a Western-style restaurant in Jacksonville, home to botanist Kumagusu Minakata for a short period of time in the early 1890s.

From around 1910, a small number of Japanese moved from the West Coast states to Florida. In about 1915, Japanese moved to St. Petersburg on Florida's Gulf Coast and opened a Japanese curio store and a Western-style restaurant there. Japanese also lived in Ft. Myers, farther south along the same coast.

At a location on the southwest shore of Lake Okeechobee in the interior of the Florida peninsula, approximately ten Japanese came in 1915 to work in the sugarcane fields. By 1919 almost all of them had left the area. Afterward, when the area became the town of Clewiston, a couple named Watanabe were all who remained. At first they worked as the servants of an American family, but from 1922 they managed the

Watanabe Hotel in Clewiston. Popular with the locals, they were affectionately called Papa and Madam Watanabe by those who lived in the area. The hotel prospered, and in 1926 it moved into a new building. However, it is believed that the Watanabes returned to Japan a year later.

Giichi Yamada, from Japan's Aichi Prefecture, first worked his way through Colorado, Kansas, Ohio, and New York, then began managing a hotel in Daytona Beach, Florida, in 1922. He moved to Miami in 1929, where he established a food distribution company together with Tomotoshi Tanaka. Also from Aichi Prefecture, Tanaka lived for a time in New York before relocating to Miami. In 1926, Sadaji Nakamura, from Tōkyō, immigrated to Miami by way of Houston, Texas.

As all of this migratory movement of Japanese was taking place, a plan was formed to settle another colony like Yamato in Florida. In 1913 anti-Japanese sentiment in California was on the rise, and a law was enacted to restrict Japanese ownership of land. At the same time, a Japanese named Seigo (Luke) Mogi was acting as an agent to sell land near Jacksonville, Florida, to California Japanese affected by the new legislation. Mogi bought and sold real estate, acted as an interpreter, and performed other related services while working out of an office in Los Angeles. The land for sale was owned by William S. Jennings, the former governor of Florida. In 1903 he had demonstrated his interest in Japanese immigration by endorsing Jo Sakai's colonization scheme that was to result in the Yamato Colony. Now, in 1913, Jennings put out the call to Japanese announcing the availability of his land near Jacksonville.

In the past, Floridians had adopted a position of tolerance toward Japanese immigration to the state. On the national stage, Democrat Woodrow Wilson, who was inaugurated as president in 1913, followed the example of his predecessor Theodore Roosevelt by opposing California's anti-Japanese legislation. William Jennings Bryan, Wilson's secretary of state and former governor Jennings's cousin, stood in the way of enacting such legislation and sought to influence California's legislature.

A celebrated orator who was also a three-time Democratic Party candidate for president, Bryan did not look favorably on increasing tensions between Japan and the United States over California's legislative agenda. In the end, though, California enacted its discriminatory leg-islation. Jennings defended his cousin's actions in the controversy and decided that it would be a good idea for Japanese no longer able to own land in California to establish themselves in Florida instead.

In response to Jennings's invitation, a group of twenty-five or so set-tlers set out for Florida in early autumn. The party reserved a train car and arrived after traveling across the continent. With Jennings offering 60,000 acres for sale, Mogi continued to recruit settlers, planning on settling as many as one hundred colonists. Learning of this migration from the West Coast, the *San Francisco Examiner*, with an anti-Japanese slant to its story, reported on the departure of the immigrants under a headline reading, "CALIFORNIA JAPS RUSH TO FLORIDA."

California Japanese who planned to go to Florida hoped to leave behind anti-Japanese sentiment and start afresh in a new location. But even in Florida they found that locals were swayed by the threat of the "yellow peril" fanned by the arrival of Japanese newcomers. Floridians expected that laws could be enacted, as they were in California, to re-strict the ownership of land by Japanese. Instead, state leaders declared that in order to do so the state constitution would have to be amended. Until that occurred, there was no way to prevent Japanese from coming to Florida.

At that point, a representative to Congress from Florida, Frank Clark, announced his opposition to Japanese immigration plans. Some newspapers, too, editorialized against Japanese immigration to Florida, calling it a "problem." Clark, who similarly described relations between whites and African Americans as a problem, presented his views on the differences between the races in a letter addressed to Florida governor Park Trammel. In it, Clark stated that because Japanese could not as-similate with the white race, he was opposed to any immigration plan for the Asians. Furthermore, Clark demanded the enactment of a law forbidding the ownership of land by Japanese.

With California's anti-Japanese movement now seeming to spread everywhere and causing agitation because of Clark's words and deeds, the Japanese government took action. In New York, Japanese con-sul general Kametarō Iijima approached Nippon Club president Dr. Jōkichi Takamine with a request. Through Takamine's brother-in-law, a congressional representative from New York, it was hoped that Clark could be persuaded to moderate his position.

In addition, Iijima wrote to Jo Sakai, who was most knowledgeable about the actual situation in Florida, seeking his opinion regarding Japanese immigration to the state. In answer, Sakai explained the circumstances at Yamato, beginning by writing about the eastern coast of Florida before the colony had been established. He explained that Henry Flagler's Florida East Coast Railway had received preferential treatment from the state that allowed Flagler to invest in and develop Florida's eastern seaboard. In as little as seventeen or eighteen years' time it had become the ideal location not only to spend the winter months, but also to grow winter vegetables.

About the establishment of the Yamato Colony itself, Sakai explained that when he was setting up the colony, people welcomed him wherever he went in Florida, with the notable exception of a group of Russian exiles. (These were the years of the Russo-Japanese War, after all.) He signed contracts with the Florida East Coast Railway, and his group immigrated to Florida under the patronage and support of the railway company. Once in Florida, the colonists took up farming, working their hardest. Unfortunately, pineapple cultivation was dealt a huge blow by favoritism shown cheaper Cuban pineapples. But in the last two or three years, the colonists' hopes for prosperity had been restored chiefly due to the efforts they put into raising winter vegetables. Some settlers had seen profits materialize right before their eyes, and although there were those who had opted to leave Yamato, the area had become known for its excellence in producing winter vegetables, Sakai explained. Furthermore, he revealed, up until that day the voice of anti-Japanese sentiment in Florida had been almost completely silent.

Mentioning that anti-Japanese activities were continuing to occur in California, Sakai then suggested that little reason existed for Japanese colonists to remain on the West Coast: "I say, why shouldn't our countrymen come to Florida, where they can demonstrate to everyone, just as we are doing here at Yamato, the true spirit of the Japanese people."

Sakai also wrote that Congressman Clark was elected with the help of the Florida East Coast Railway, and that his qualifications as a congressman were questionable. About Mogi's plan to bring Japanese colonists to Florida, Sakai wrote that while he welcomed the arrival of self-sufficient farmers, it was wrong that Mogi was selling land to such buyers with no thought given to their success, only for the sake of making money from the land sales. Furthermore, Sakai pointed out, if the intended location of Mogi's settlement, as identified in his plans, was somewhere that no one could hope to develop, then the success of his plans was in doubt.

Both the Japanese embassy in Washington and the consulate general in New York contacted the home office for advice, and on October 17 they heard about the situation from Mogi himself. With encouragement from them, Mogi halted further emigration from California in order to avoid additional public scrutiny and not make matters worse. He submitted a report in which he indicated that, for the moment, the only crops being planted by the Japanese consisted of potatoes, and that if planting occurred in winter, there was no need to call for additional immigrants until the end of April. For the time being, only eight were necessary to tend to the crops.

Mogi's settlement was called the Middleburg Colony, taking its name from the town near the colony site. There, Mogi's settlers cleared land and planted crops. But the quality of the soil and means for transporting their harvest proved problematic. In only a short period of time few families remained, and the colony ended in failure. The Middleburg settlers moved to the Jacksonville suburbs or to the Japanese settlements at Eau Gallie and Yamato, while also relocating out of state to places other than California. The fate of the Middleburg Colony was exactly as Sakai had predicted in his report to Consul General Iijima.

A Fresh Start

Morikami Enrolls in Elementary School

Yamato settlers who had given up on a future in Florida left the colony, while others stayed and created families. For Morikami, returning to Japan, marrying, and bringing a wife back to the United States as some settlers did was hardly an option. Morikami worried that he would not receive the $500 bonus that Mitsusaburo Oki had promised him, and when he did not, he had to resign himself to making a life in America. "I couldn't go back [to Japan]. I had no money. The only thing I could do was stay here and do something." He remembered his uneasiness about the future. While almost all of the members of the colony were educated and understood English, Morikami had never studied the language and hardly knew a word.

Morikami thought the best plan for him to learn English was to hire himself out to an American family as live-in domestic help, so he ran a classified ad in a newspaper for such a position. As a result, he went to work for a boatbuilder in Eau Gallie, a coastal town about 120 miles north of the Japanese colony. However, the work, which paid ten dollars per month, consisted of long hours of backbreaking physical labor that left almost no opportunity to practice his English language skills.

Sukeji (George) Morikami as a young man, ca. 1909 (courtesy Morikami Museum and Japanese Gardens).

Morikami soon changed his mind about the best way to learn English and decided to attend classes instead. To earn money for such a purpose, he quit his job with the boatbuilder and, renting a little land outside of town, started a small farm.

Harvesting a crop of cabbage, turnips, and tomatoes, Morikami put them into a gunnysack that had originally held a couple hundred pounds of fertilizer. Filling the sack with the newly picked vegetables, he slung it over his shoulder and peddled his vegetables door-to-door, walking weed-choked paths for over forty miles, sinking into the loose sand with each step. Fresh vegetables were scarce, especially in summertime, he later said. He had no difficulty in selling them because so few were available.

However, Morikami was unable to save enough money in this way to pay for classes and study English. He gave up on hawking vegetables around town and thought instead, Why not study at the local elementary school for a year? He asked the school whether he could attend classes.

At first school administrators and the school board voiced objections, but Minoru Ohi, a Japanese who operated a farm in Eau Gallie and originally had been a member of the Yamato Colony, went to the school and explained how much Morikami desired to learn. He also noted that Morikami only wanted to study the same curriculum as the other students. Thanks to Ohi's intervention, Morikami was allowed to attend the school. Boarding with Ohi, he began classes as a fifth-grade pupil.

Thus, a twenty-three-year-old Japanese took his seat beside American children attending school. Although short in stature, he looked out of place beside his schoolmates because of his features and physique. The children looked on this foreign adult who sat beside them with wide-eyed curiosity. But with his characteristic smiling face and friendly demeanor, Morikami was soon accepted as one of them.

Acting as Morikami's "guardian," Ohi inspected the report card that Morikami brought to him at the end of each school term. For Morikami, school was a most challenging experience, although his grades were always excellent. In this way he was able to acquire a foundation in the English language as well as learn about American culture.

Meanwhile, Morikami received news from home that Hatsu Onizawa, the young woman to whom he had once proposed, had married someone else. Hatsu, having attained the age of eighteen, had married a young man from Miyazu who worked for Japan National Railways. Morikami learned that the marriage had been arranged by the parents of the young couple. Now that there was no more talk of a $500 bonus, Morikami could not but give up on returning to Japan, much less tendering a proposal of marriage. He felt his shoulders sag even more as he thought, "It is always the person for whom you yearn most that is beyond your reach."

A Big Harvest on Borrowed Land

Morikami returned to the Yamato Colony a year later. There, tomatoes and winter vegetables were being grown following the failure of the pineapple. Market prices were satisfactory, and profits were on the rise. Morikami, who was allowed to stay in a shack that Jo Sakai owned, began growing vegetables. Because he had neither ready cash nor land, Morikami asked a friend whether he could use his help. The friend agreed to loan Morikami the use of a half acre of land, which he immediately set about clearing.

The plot was as much as one person could farm with a hoe, a rake, and a shovel. He recalled the friend telling him, "You finish the clearing and plant and raise the crop, and no charge for the rent." However, Morikami did not have money to buy seeds or fertilizer, so he approached a store run by an American.

He wanted "to do a little farming," Morikami told the shopkeeper, who he hoped would advance him enough to eat until he had sent his crop to market. Responding to Morikami's request, the merchant acted generously. "I don't know you, but your country people seem honest," he said. "All right. I'll let you have all the food and the groceries that you need and you can pay me back when the crops are ready."

Thanks to the shopkeeper's munificence Morikami was able to procure all that he needed day to day, including shirts and pants. As for fertilizer, when Morikami negotiated with the authorized agent representing the one company that served the state, he was allowed the same terms: when the harvest came in, he could then settle his account.

Morikami was also given the use of a spare room rent-free at the house of the friend who loaned him use of the land on which he raised his crop. Finally, he bought some tools—a hoe (at $1.25), an ax ($1.50), a shovel ($1.25), and a galvanized bucket ($0.25). Morikami could not stretch his money far enough to buy a wheelbarrow, however. When it came time to ship his produce, he had no means of getting it to the packinghouse other than carrying it over his shoulder. He put the produce into a gunnysack with the capacity to hold 200 pounds, and half carried, half dragged it, using up a lot of time in the process. The load was so heavy that when he stopped carrying the sack, Morikami could not take another step. As a result, the first thing he did when he had the cash in hand was buy a wheelbarrow.

That first season was quite rainy, Morikami remembered, with precipitation over long periods of time making his work that much more difficult. With so much rain, the crop was in danger of flooding. His field, though, was close to a canal, which was ideal for drainage. Furthermore, when he prepared his field at the beginning of the season he built the earth up into high ridges, planting a row of seedlings down the middle of each one. By leaving a two-and-a-half-foot space between each ridge, Morikami prevented the field from flooding. Because of the care he took in planting his crop, the results come harvesttime were outstanding.

That season yielded an especially fine crop of tomatoes, green with no sign of disease or worms. In one day Morikami was able to pick eighty-four bushels' worth. "Eighty-four, and without help," he proudly recalled many years later. When the newly picked tomatoes were taken to the packinghouse, packed, and shipped to market, they sold for the very highest prices, estimated to be around $224 for the eighty-four bushels. At the end of the season, after expenses, Morikami had in hand $1,000 for his crop. For his efforts, he took home an amount that was twice that of the bonus that he was never able to collect. This success was in 1912, six years since he had come to America.

A Mail-Order Business Brings Success

Morikami, who showed what he could do on borrowed farmland, soon began buying land of his own a little at a time. Since he did not always buy parcels that were contiguous with one another, he owned a number of isolated fields that were scattered here and there, some of them having sold for as little as fifteen dollars per acre. He even bought land from other settlers who were returning to Japan. Hiring five or six African American field hands to help, he started farming for the first time on land of his own.

To sell the crops he harvested, Morikami tried something new. Up to that time it had been customary for farmers to sell their crops to agents acting as middlemen who had complete discretion over decisions regarding shipping arrangements and selling the produce at market. Agents worked with each farmer individually, so it was unclear just how much they were making in commissions.

Later, agents, rather than growers, sent quotations for quantities and prices of produce to preferred customers every week. To restaurants, hotels, and neighborhood groceries they sent lists indicating how much tomatoes, beans, and other produce weighed, what they cost, and how soon they could be shipped. The customer, looking at this quotation, ordered produce by mail. A middleman was still involved in the process. But this way, a farmer's profits were easier to estimate accurately than they had been when commission agents controlled the shipment and sales of produce. Morikami discovered that the middleman realized a profit of one dollar for each basket of produce sold.

As a result, Morikami determined that he would try to get orders directly from the potential customers himself. He went to a local bank and borrowed the *Blue Book* for the southern states, listing preferred credit risks to whom he could market his produce. He studied the thick, heavy volume over a period of two or three weeks, picking out the names and addresses and making a mailing list of around 300 people throughout the South who might be suitable customers.

Morikami then prepared a postcard with a reply card attached. On one side of a perforated line he listed prices and provided other information about the produce he had to offer. On the other side of the perforation he printed an order form to fill out and return. His total cost was only the price of the postcard. The first order Morikami received was for five crates of tomatoes, but from this beginning the numbers of orders gradually increased, and soon they came from over half of the addresses to which he sent cards. The volume of business that came to him was evidence of how much his customers esteemed the quality of his produce.

Morikami, who had adopted the American name George, called his business George S. Morikami Company. Not stopping in the South alone, his list of names grew to include other regions of the country as well. Orders came from the West Coast states of California and Washington, and even from Alaska. His shipments began their journeys on the Florida East Coast Railway, later utilizing the network of railroads that crisscrossed the United States. Every day at 3:00 p.m., Morikami sent off a shipment of produce from Yamato Station on the express arriving from Miami.

This process went on for a period of three or four years. Morikami profited handsomely, and the savings in his bank account steadily increased. His life changed dramatically; he did well enough to afford the cost of staying in an upscale hotel and eating his meals there. But as orders from customers kept increasing, stress began to weigh on Morikami. When orders came in, he had to make arrangements to ship the produce, and sometimes there was no produce to ship.

Morikami felt the responsibility to respond to orders he received no matter what, and he bought produce from other farmers to ship to his customers. As hardships piled up, his health deteriorated and he developed a severe stomach ulcer. Yet somehow Morikami's business continued, and he kept increasing his landholdings by buying a few acres at a time. At just about that time the Florida real estate boom of the 1920s began.

The Florida Real Estate Boom
and Its Collapse

Riding the Overseas Railroad to Key West

At the time that the Yamato Colony was established, development all over the state of Florida was poised to take off. Construction of the railroad extension to Key West, which had begun in 1905, proceeded smoothly where it was being built on land, but experienced difficulties where it was being built over water.

As construction progressed, workers were sought from all over: from elsewhere in the United States, from Cuba, from the West Indies, and from the Cayman Islands. At any given time as many as 3,000 men were working on-site. To build bridge piers, the workers constructed watertight cofferdams, drove pilings into the bedrock inside of them, pumped out water and mud, and poured cement in around the pilings. The right quality of cement for this purpose could only be imported from Germany.

On top of having to work in strong winds and rough surf, workers were subjected to the occasional hurricane. Construction of the railroad was set back considerably by one hurricane in particular that struck in 1906, the year that George Morikami came to Florida. Winds with speeds that reached 125 miles per hour demolished barges sheltering workers who were building spans over the open water. Seventy men were blown out to sea, their remains never recovered. Some of those who were saved were found at sea hundreds of miles away.

Learning from this hurricane, company officials put preventive measures in place that minimized damage from hurricanes that followed. Although construction was delayed in part as a result of such storms, Flagler was able at last to realize his dream of a rail link between Key West and peninsular Florida on January 21, 1912.

Commemorating this tremendous achievement, the first passenger train to run the full length of the Overseas Railroad arrived in Key West at 10:43 a.m. the following day, January 22. Thousands of people, including Key West residents, thronged the station, raising a cry as they met the train. Spanish mingled with French among the voices of those who had come from various parts of the Caribbean.

Off the train stepped Henry Flagler, architect of the grand plan that resulted in the Overseas Railroad. He was followed by a number of company officials for whom an elaborate reception was held. Announcing the completion of the railroad, the *Miami Herald* newspaper called it the Eighth Wonder of the World.

In this way, the United States was linked by rail all along the Atlantic coast from New England in the North to the country's southernmost point. The railroad's terminal was near the pier in Key West. From there, passengers transferring to steamships could go on to Havana, Cuba.

A train called the Havana Special departed from Boston in the evening. It made stops in New York and Washington, DC, entered Florida after passing through the Carolinas and Georgia, and arrived in Key West at noon on the third day in transit. Passengers from the Havana Special continued their journey aboard a steamship leaving Key West before noon of the following day, disembarking at the port of Havana by evening.

On May 20, 1913, a year after the completion of his railroad extension to Key West, Henry Morrison Flagler passed away at age eighty-three at his home in Palm Beach.

Japanese Participate in the Development of Miami Beach

Development in southern Florida did not stop with Flagler's death but continued in the most iconic location of all, Miami Beach. In 1896, when the Florida East Coast Railway first reached Miami, hotels sprang up there as the city became a popular place to spend the winter. Then real estate development began on a large scale on Miami Beach, a barrier island east of Miami on the other side of Biscayne Bay.

The first to begin developing Miami Beach was business entrepreneur Carl Fisher. Originally from Indianapolis, Fisher became involved in the development of the famous Indianapolis Motor Speedway and later realized a plan to complete the coast-to-coast road called the Lincoln Highway. In 1910 he took advantage of a trip to Miami to begin developing Miami Beach, then nothing more than a sandbar in its natural state. Fisher acquired property, removed trees, and prepared the land for construction. Making use of fill acquired by dredging, he leveled the ground and sold land divided into residential lots. Keeping pace with these improvements, he paved roads and built hotels. As his goal was constructing a playground for society's upper crust, he planted coconut palms lining the streets that crisscrossed the island and also planned exclusive shopping venues.

The Overseas Railroad through the Florida Keys at the Seven Mile Bridge (courtesy Florida State Archives).

A view of early Miami Beach, ca. 1920: the windmill at Carl Fisher's Roman Pools and Casino (courtesy Yoko Tashiro).

In order to recruit competent people to realize his plans for development, Fisher ran newspaper advertisements. Japanese laborer Shigezo Tashiro, who lived in San Francisco, was among those who responded to these ads. Tashiro was from Minami Ashigara in Kanagawa Prefecture, where his family's business had been in sericulture. As the business faltered, though, Tashiro's father ended up deeply in debt. Because of this, Shigezo decided in 1899 to travel to San Francisco with his older brother Chotaro, saying, "In Japan it would take a lifetime to get back everything we have lost, but in America we can easily earn the money that we need."

Once in the United States, the brothers worked a variety of jobs, from farm labor to railroad work to landscape gardening. They saved up their money and inside of a year were able to pay off their family's debt in Japan. Seeing the advertisement in the newspaper, the Tashiro brothers secured positions by writing to Fisher. They left San Francisco shortly afterward and traveled to Florida, where they began working for Fisher in 1916. Although later the Tashiros got to know George Morikami, at the time they had no idea of the existence of the Yamato Colony, some forty-five or fifty miles north of Miami Beach.

After the Tashiros arrived in Miami Beach they got in touch with Ko-taro Suto, a friend they had known in San Francisco, and he, too, got a job working for Carl Fisher in Florida. Fisher, who sought to make the most of his new employees' landscape gardening skills, entrusted them with planting trees and other tasks associated with his plan to develop a garden oasis by the sea in Miami Beach. The Tashiros removed man-groves that grew in profusion at the water's edge, worked hard to dig out the scrub palmettos, roots and all, and then leveled the ground with bulldozers. They also dredged the ocean bottom and accumulated fill to create more land. Moreover, the Tashiro brothers did the landscap-ing for hotels, polo grounds, golf courses, and residential communities. After a while, Shigezo Tashiro took over as supervisor of landscaping for the real estate company being run by Fisher, who regarded his work highly.

After working for Carl Fisher for about four years, Shigezo left the company to strike out on his own. With older brother Chotaro, he es-tablished a business, Miami Beach Nurseries, to engage in horticulture and landscape gardening in the city of Miami Beach. He ran the com-pany, raised plants, and for the first time sold plants to the public. Be-fore long Chotaro returned to Japan, while Shigezo stayed to manage the company.

Gradually Miami Beach attracted the wealthy, and Tashiro under-took more and more jobs at large mansions, among them the prop-erty owned by William K. Vanderbilt II, a member of the prominent Vanderbilt family.

Palm Beach, Miami, Miami Beach—these were places in southern Florida where development had taken off. They were beads on a string that would provide the basis for a densely populated urban area. Even farming regions like Yamato would soon be caught up in the real es-tate boom that the development of these resort communities had anticipated.

The Newspaper Puts Out a 504-Page Publication

In the 1920s, the Florida real estate market heated up to an unprec-edented degree. With incomes on the rise as the result of economic growth in the US, people working in the nation's urban areas took advantage of paid vacations to get away from their everyday lives characterized mostly by hard work and austerity. The spread of privately owned automobiles gave impetus to this movement.

Northerners who lived in cities like New York rushed to Florida for the warm climate. Regarded primarily as a resort area, southern Florida inspired visitors to view the region not only as a travel destination but also as an attractive place in which to spend the winter. It aroused people's desires to own property there but also encouraged them to speculate in the real estate market. Until then, those who had traveled to Florida were the elderly, the wealthy, and the ailing needing to convalesce. Starting in the 1920s, more and more visitors were middle-class families. Hotels and casinos were subsequently built to accommodate these newcomers, with structures—indeed, entire developments—finished to resemble the look of Southern California or a Mediterranean style mimicking the Riviera.

Ordinary individuals looking to purchase real estate could buy on credit if they did not have the requisite capital. While many wanted to own homes in Florida and live lives of luxury, most hoped only to make a profit through the resale of their property. This was evident from the fact that two-thirds of the real estate sold in Florida was not purchased by buyers who visited the state, but was sold through the mail for the purpose of speculation.

In Florida, cars bearing license plates from many different states could be seen everywhere. At the same time, real estate salesmen spoke of the railroad's future plans and of streets where none had yet been built, thereby fanning the flames of speculation fever among buyers. In Miami Beach, the price of the land changed by the hour. Stories of property that had sold for $10 thirty years ago currently selling for $100,000 were heard over and over again. With real estate advertising taking up more space in newspapers such as the *Miami Herald*, the *Miami Daily News* went so far as to publish an advertising supplement the size of a 500-page telephone book in the summer of 1925.

Even in the vicinity of Yamato, about forty-five miles north of Miami, the price of land was increasing. Advertisements for the sale of real estate, like one reading, "YAMATO 90 ACRES—Price $1000 Per Acre," appeared frequently in the newspaper. Several Yamato settlers bought and sold property during the real estate boom, even selling their farm fields, then leaving Florida for other states. After selling much of his land, Oscar Kobayashi first stayed in Florida to try poultry raising as a business. A short time later, though, he disposed of the remainder of his property and moved to the Chicago area.

Considering the negative aspects of farming in southern Florida—outdoor work, rising property taxes—perhaps selling off one's land and leaving Yamato was a sound choice to make. For those owning property, incentives to continue farming were rapidly diminishing. What is more, the time had passed when educated men needed to farm the land in order to make a living, as the Yamato settlers had done during the colony's early days. Now, the colony that Jo Sakai had envisioned, a colony dependent on the farm fields those settlers had cleared, was disappearing little by little as the colonists succumbed to easy money from the sale of their land.

The Collapse of Sakai's Dream

Sakai himself could not continue his enterprise for reasons of health. On June 9, 1923, Sakai and Henry Kamiya learned from a brother that their mother, who lived in Miyazu, had passed away. Then, on the twenty-first of the following month, while taking a bath after returning home from work, Sakai began coughing up blood. He went to a doctor, but he afterward coughed up blood again, this time more of it than before.

Beginning about ten years after the Yamato Colony was first settled, illness had overcome Sakai a number of times. Every time it occurred, he recovered after resting, but this time was different—he had contracted tuberculosis. Sakai's condition was more serious than it had ever been. Ten days after spitting up blood he entered a sanatorium in Asheville, North Carolina, accompanied by a doctor to monitor his medical treatment closely.

Despite such care, after three weeks at the sanatorium Sakai passed away at the age of forty-seven on August 21, 1923. It was eleven days before the Great Kantō Earthquake would strike Japan, devastating Tōkyō and Yokohama. Sakai, his wife, Sada, and their five daughters were members of the Delray Methodist Church, where a Christian funeral was held.

The house in Yamato in which the Sakai, and later the Kamiya, families resided, ca. 1940 (courtesy Morikami Museum and Japanese Gardens).

Sakai, who wore glasses and a moustache on a long, narrow face, had the look of an intellectual. As seen by the members of his family, he was serious and hardworking, not the sort of person who smiled easily. Foremost in his mind at all times was what was necessary for the growth of the colony.

In addition to their firstborn son, who died shortly after he was born, the Sakais had five daughters. Their second daughter, Tomo, had only one memory of her always serious-minded father that gave the impression that he was also a compassionate, gentle man. She was about five years old at the time. She and her sisters were on their way to Japan, where they were being taken for a yearlong visit, when she was stricken with a case of diphtheria and admitted to a hospital in Chicago. Tomo hovered between life and death, unconscious for several days. When at last she regained consciousness, she saw her father at the foot of her bed with his face buried in his hands. After a moment, when Jo noticed that Tomo had opened her eyes, the look of relief on his face was evident.

Three days after his death, Sakai's remains were interred at Woodlawn Cemetery in West Palm Beach. The cemetery, in which the Sakais' eldest son, Hiroshi, also lay in repose, had been created by Henry Flagler. In death as in life, Sakai continued to occupy land made available by the developer and railroad tycoon.

With her husband's death, Sada resolved to return to Japan, deciding that remaining at Yamato and raising the couple's children there by herself presented too many difficulties. Shortly thereafter, she started out on her long journey together with her five daughters. Of them, only her oldest daughter, Chikako, who was enrolled in high school in Delray, was reluctant to leave Florida.

Nor did other colony settlers remain long after the death of Jo Sakai, whose tenure as colony leader had lasted a couple of decades. The family of Oscar Kobayashi, for example, departed in 1925, leaving Yamato for the estate of Col. George Fabyan in Geneva, Illinois. Among the Japanese who remained, Henry Kamiya, Jo Sakai's younger brother, assumed a leadership role in community affairs.

Kamiya and his wife, Yetsu, had a total of six children, three boys and three girls. The oldest daughter was Masako, followed by Mishiko, sons Rokuo and Takamichi, youngest daughter Masuko, and youngest son Kazuo. The six of them were given Japanese names and at the same time English names as well, although only Takamichi was better known by his English name of Franklin or Frank.

Besides raising vegetables, Kamiya opened a store in Yamato offering groceries and sundries. Because his store was patronized by everyone living in the area, the colonists naturally tended to regard him as a community leader. Kamiya lived in a large two-story house, had an outgoing personality, drove an automobile, rode a motorcycle, and enjoyed fishing. Moreover, he enjoyed sports and built a tennis court on his property. He was also adored by his children, through whom he had a link to everyone in the vicinity, not just to the Japanese.

Kamiya managed employees working his extensive farm fields, often joining them in doing much of the everyday farm labor himself. He participated in planting, fertilizing, and harvesting, and he helped take the necessary measures to assure that his crops received adequate water, including digging ditches. When Japanese guests came from afar to visit Yamato, the Kamiya house was always open to them. In December 1921, the various households in the colony—the Sakais, the Ashidas, the Yamauchis, and others—got together there for a lively Christmas party. A week later, on New Year's Day, almost everyone in the colony paid a courtesy visit to the Kamiya family to commemorate the holiday.

On New Year's Day 1923, eighteen Yamato residents got together, including the Sakai family, Shikazo and Shizuyo Ashida, Yonehachi Mori, and Shohbi Kamikama, among others. Sometimes George Morikami would show up at Kamiya's house to talk about work or buying or selling one or the other's property. When Morikami developed stomach ulcers, Kamiya came to see him to ask about his health.

Kamiya's life was not without problems, however. In 1914, the Kamiya house burned to the ground one evening when the family was out. The cause of the fire was determined to be a lantern that had been left unattended. In short order, though, Kamiya got together with a carpenter to make plans for rebuilding. The death of his brother, Jo Sakai, was also a blow. Furthermore, Kamiya's business interests gradually required greater austerity in management, and in 1925 he sold off a portion of his real estate holdings. As the economy teetered on the edge of recession, Kamiya's finances were also in distress.

Morikami Achieves Wealth but Is Bankrupt Overnight

Through much of 1925 it was apparent that the real estate boom was beginning to falter. Speculators who purchased property with the sole intention of selling it at a profit found that they were unable to do so, leaving them with debt and land of little value. In the summer of 1926, symptoms of a sharp decline in the real estate market appeared. Three banks in Delray, near Yamato, shut their doors, and crowds gathered outside to demand the return of their savings.

As this was happening, a major hurricane made landfall in Miami on September 18. It destroyed houses and reduced whole city blocks to rubble. Resort hotels were damaged beyond recognition. Around 400 people lost their lives. The Kamiya house, too, shook in the strong winds during the night. Windows shattered and glass flew, while a large tree near the house crashed to the ground. Authorities in southern Florida estimated total damages amounting to $200 million.

Banks in large urban centers like Miami, Jacksonville, and Tampa continued to operate, but local banks—those near Yamato—all failed, shuttering their doors for good. For several years after that, many more banks went bankrupt. With local financial institutions failing, the Yamato settlers could not help but be affected. George Morikami was one of them.

Morikami had been saving the money he made from running his mail-order business even while suffering from ulcers. At the same time, he continued to buy and sell real estate, increasing his personal assets. Taking advantage of rising land prices during the real estate boom, Morikami purchased land for as little as $100, then sold it for $4,000 two years later. Furthermore, he invested in bank stocks, lumber companies, and the hotel business, watching his profits rise. Thus Morikami became a wealthy man. He had altogether around $250,000 deposited in bank accounts at five different banks, owned two or three automobiles, and generally, in his own words, "put on the airs of a millionaire" (*daijin-kaze o fukasete orimashita* 大尽風を吹かせて居りました).

Around this time Morikami got to know a young American woman of German ancestry. He decided to propose marriage to this eighteen-year-old, who worked as a secretary for a farm produce distribution company, and in the summer of 1924 he constructed a $6,000 California-style bungalow near downtown Delray for them to move into. Viewed from the front, the house had a roof with gently sloping eaves. It was around thirty feet long on a side and sturdily built. Two weeks before it was to be completed, however, Morikami's young fiancé died suddenly of illness. In despair, he sold the house and went to live for a time at the Kentucky House, the earliest resort hotel in Delray Beach.

Later, reflecting on this time in his life when he had the means to live at the Kentucky House, Morikami recognized the truth in the Japanese proverb "Bad luck follows good" (*kōji maōshi* 好事魔多し). Because of the collapse of the real estate bubble in 1926, the banks in which Morikami had deposited his savings failed, and economic depression in Florida followed. Morikami lost everything.

As a result of the bank closures, Morikami found himself unable to cover even his daily expenses. At that point he decided to resume his mail-order business, but he first went around to financial institutions over a period of a couple of weeks in order to obtain a loan. Happily, he was able to secure a $5,000 loan and after five months quickly made close to $5,000 in profit.

After the Florida real estate boom, the public's mania for speculative behavior turned to the stock market instead, causing the prices of shares to rise sharply. Then, on October 24, 1929, Black Thursday touched off financial panic and the Great Depression. Not long afterward, Florida further felt the impact of the widespread failure of the banking system. Call him lucky, but Morikami had nothing more to lose.

The mail-order farm-produce business that Morikami had taken up again made the transition smoothly to the new economic realities, and he made money despite the hard times. However, his personal situation ended up no different than it had been previously. In order to fill orders, he had to buy produce from other farmers, cutting into his profit margin. This caused the buildup of stress, and the ulcers that he had suffered once before returned.

On the day of Christmas Eve 1932, Morikami went out to his fields as usual. Stopping to talk to one of his sharecroppers, he collapsed on the ground, spitting up blood. When he could not get to his feet, a doctor was called. "If you want to live," the doctor told him, "you must go to a hospital in Miami at once."

Although Morikami disliked hospitals, he had no alternative but to find one and check himself in. No sooner was he admitted than he underwent an operation. During the procedure, which began around ten o'clock that evening, doctors removed nearly half of his stomach. Afterward Morikami slept fifteen hours as if he were dead. When he had almost completely recovered a couple of months later, the doctor told Morikami to quit the mail-order business that was making him ill, and from that day forward he devoted himself to no more than working in his fields. After the operation, he wrote to Yoneji, his youngest sibling, in Japan, telling him of the ordeal. If Morikami was looking for sympathy, he did not find it in his brother, who told him instead, "[Your illness] was a curse for your lack of filial devotion to our parents."

As for Henry Kamiya, who relied on loans to keep his farming business afloat, the financial panic of 1929 affected his operation in no small measure. Among other misfortunes that his family suffered, Kamiya's eldest son, Rokuo, who had just turned seventeen on June 15 of that year, was thrown from his motorcycle. Hitting his head, he lost consciousness for a time and was taken to a hospital. He regained consciousness shortly afterward and seemed to be recovering, but because he appeared pale despite having taken medicine, Kamiya gave him a shot of whiskey. Rokuo subsequently lost consciousness again and passed away that evening.

"I should have let him lie quietly," Kamiya wrote in his diary. "I had him drink whiskey instead of using ice to keep his fever down, and it stimulated his blood flow. Because of that, his blood vessel ended up bursting. I feel so guilty that I killed my son. I am in such pain. I feel so sorry for him."

Although the year ended unhappily for Kamiya with the loss of his eldest son, during the 1930 New Year's observance the families of other Yamato settlers—Jinzo Yamauchi, Hideo Kobayashi, and Gengoro Yoshida, among others—paid courtesy visits and joined the Kamiyas in sharing a holiday meal. In 1931, too, the Yamato Japanese again made New Year's courtesy calls on a number of the households in the community, especially that of the Kamiyas.

News of the Japanese invasion of Manchuria and of unrest in Japan gradually reached Kamiya from around this time. In April 1932, staff members of the Japanese consulate in New Orleans paid a visit of inspection to Yamato, and in July 1933, the Kamiyas attended the World's Exposition in Chicago. Kamiya's lifestyle left him some spare time, even though between hiring employees and working in his farm fields he always seemed to be chasing down financing. He applied for farm loans and discussed borrowing money from friends.

Kamiya often had to deal with crop damage from heavy rainfall and storms as well as long periods of drought. In the autumn of 1934, for example, the heat was particularly severe, and day after day went by when no one could work.

The Fates of Japanese Colonies in Texas and California

The Japanese colonies in Texas, which began operation around the same time as Yamato, underwent changes similar to those of their Florida counterpart. At the Kishi Colony, which Kichimatsu Kishi had established east of Houston in 1908, settlers initially focused on cultivating rice but later switched to growing vegetables. They hired workers with various ethnic backgrounds, including Mexicans, African Americans, and Europeans, as well as Japanese.

In 1919, oil was discovered on Kishi's property, and he quickly set up the Orange Petroleum Company. As a result, Isoroku Yamamoto visited the Kishi Colony while making a tour of oil-producing facilities. By the beginning of World War II, Yamamoto would become supreme commander of the Japanese imperial fleet, but in 1919 he was a student at Harvard University. The house in which Yamamoto was born in Nagaoka, Niigata Prefecture, was quite close to Kishi's childhood home, and Yamamoto's brother knew someone who was a friend of Kishi's. Looking to Japan's future, Yamamoto, who was interested in oil as a natural resource, made visits to the Kishi Colony on a couple of occasions over several years while inspecting oil production sites.

The Kishi family actively sought to assimilate into the local community, and Kishi tried to return profits from his business to the local economy whenever possible. In 1924 he donated land for a community church, had the church constructed, and even contributed funds for its operation. He also transferred ownership of a parcel of land to a school located near the colony site in 1928. Although he himself was a Buddhist, Kishi taught his children to accept the Christian faith and to learn English since they were to live in America.

Kishi sold his company after his oil wells stopped producing. With profits from the sale he is said to have repaid colony investors three times their initial investment. At the same time, he continued to buy land and enlarge the colony, which he oversaw according to modern methods of management. In this way the enterprise underwent changes without difficulties, although it was not long before problems began to stack up.

The cabbage crop developed lethal yellowing of the leaves, while other crops suffered terribly from cold weather and other causes. Unfortunately, the stock market crash and nationwide financial panic quickly came on the heels of this calamity. Unable to pay back funds he had borrowed to expand his business, Kishi lost 9,000 acres of his land to creditors in 1931.

According to state law at the time, Kishi was permitted to retain 200 acres for his private residence, which would be exempted from use in satisfying his debts. He refused this, however, and used proceeds from the sale of the property to help pay off every cent he owed. Kishi's Japanese employees left him and went elsewhere looking for places to make a living, some remaining in Texas, others not. In this way the Kishi Colony quietly disappeared, leaving only a cemetery behind where some former colony members are interred.

Seitō Saibara, who purchased land outside of Houston, Texas, in 1903 and established a farm there, applied for American citizenship soon afterward. His application was denied, though, as a result of opposition to Japanese immigration. Despairing of becoming naturalized, Saibara turned his attention to Brazil and left the United States.

Entrusting the management of the farm to his eldest son, Kiyoaki, Saibara left his family behind in Texas and traveled by himself to Sao Paulo. There he battled hardships for fifteen years, finally returning to Texas for a short period of time. He subsequently moved on to Taiwan, where he had financial interests in another farming enterprise. Saibara then returned to Japan, but in his later years he sought the care of his son's family in Texas. At the farm cooperative there, Kiyoaki passed on its leadership to a new generation while maintaining good relationships with the local community and working to enlarge the scope of the business.

In California, the Yamato Colony, which consisted of a cooperative association and Japanese-operated farms, actively sought to reduce anti-Japanese sentiment expressed toward its inhabitants. One measure the colonists took was to build a Christian church, which even Buddhist members of the colony helped to construct. The church became a focal point of the community. Furthermore, members of the colony refrained from opening their own retail businesses, except for those selling farm produce, in order to avoid competition with white-owned stores in nearby towns. Successful in maintaining amicable relationships with the wider community, the colony itself has continued to exist to this day.

The Demise of the Colony

A Powerful Hurricane Destroys the Overseas Railroad

For as long as humans have lived in Florida, they have struggled with the force of hurricanes. In the autumn of 1935, several major hurricanes advanced on southern Florida in quick succession, one striking the Florida Keys on Saturday, September 2—Labor Day.

In 1928, the author Ernest Hemingway visited Key West with his second wife. Shortly afterward, he built a house there where he lived while writing some of his best-known novels. Around four o'clock in the afternoon of September 2, 1935, Hemingway finished his writing for the day and sat down to look through the evening paper. The weather was typical for late summer in Key West: the temperature was approximately 80° with clear skies and a breeze off of the ocean.

However, the US Weather Bureau had already issued a hurricane warning for all of the Keys, from Key West north to Key Largo. The barometer suddenly began to fall, and the wind and rain came up with increasing intensity. Violent, tornado-like winds with speeds exceeding 150 miles per hour soon hammered the Middle Keys. Classified as a category five hurricane today, the 1935 storm whipped up sand with such fury that it tore the clothing off of anyone who happened to be outside.

At the time, a crew of 650 World War I veterans were constructing the Overseas Highway in the Florida Keys as part of President Franklin D. Roosevelt's New Deal programs. Seeking to provide employment for destitute veterans, the government put them to work building the highway beside the Overseas Railroad that Henry Flagler had completed in 1912. The government provided housing for the veterans in three encampments near Islamorada, at the southern end of the Upper Keys. Authorities in Miami dispatched a train to evacuate the servicemen, but it was unable to reach them. As the hurricane bore down on the work camps, it pounded them with storm surge, which also swept the rescue train from the tracks. Although the crew of the train survived, 259 veterans perished in the storm.

The Overseas Railroad, on which Henry Flagler had expended considerable capital, labor, and time, was reduced to splinters and washed away. Embankments were washed out for miles, and rails had been torn from their foundations and left as twisted wreckage, some of it carried great distances by the storm surge. In this hurricane that demolished bridges and buildings, 408 people succumbed in the Florida Keys alone.

With potential investors facing the prospect of economic stagnation for years to come after the stock market crash, no one had the means or the inclination to invest in the reconstruction of the Overseas Railroad. Developing a means of traveling to Key West other than by ship would have to wait until the highway was completed.

The Colonists Depart

Luckily, neither Boca Raton nor Delray Beach was affected by this hurricane, but a storm two months later on November 4 caused damage to Kamiya's fields. "Wind speed, 86 miles [per hour], up from 60 miles per hour at five o'clock. . . . Crops almost completely destroyed due to the strong northeasterly wind; seed beds, too, at the same time," Kamiya entered in his diary for that day. The following day he again bemoaned the extent of the damage: "Today is truly too terrible for me to look around. Nothing was spared. From what I see, I wonder if it is even worth the trouble of getting to work and starting over." He continued, writing of his difficult financial circumstances, "From the end of last month, the banks have been short of cash. At home, we don't even have a single dollar."

In January 1936, as the new year dawned, Kamiya's wife, Yetsu, passed away at the age of fifty-four. Her funeral was held at a church in Delray Beach, and she was buried in the cemetery in West Palm Beach where her eldest son, Rokuo, and brother-in-law, Jo Sakai, had also been laid to rest.

At the same time, something odd, possibly relating to the then-current political situation in Japan, occurred in Florida: Soon after New Year's 1936, three Japanese military officers stationed overseas made what appeared to be a purposeful visit to the southern region of the state. While the presence of these officers was of little consequence for Japanese in other parts of the US, their visit did involve residents of Yamato. Kamiya recorded the curious incident in his diary. As the military men sat down to a meal together with him and others of the colony, they quizzed their hosts for information—as if spying on the United States!

Kamiya also recorded events in his diary that affected his life indirectly, like the Japanese Army's attempted coup in Japan. Known as the February 26 Incident, it occurred shortly after the Japanese military officers' visit to Yamato but was otherwise unrelated to that event. Kamiya revealed in his diary that basic facts regarding the 1936 incident reached him quickly. The news unsettled him, making him feel as if open revolt had broken out in Japan. Then, three years later in 1939, Germany invaded Poland. In his diary, Kamiya confided his fear that Germany was moving the world closer to war. He also used the diary to record the final visit to Yamato by officials of the Japanese government. In February 1941, Kamiya spent a half day entertaining a Mr. Ōtsuka and other members of the staff of the Japanese Railroad Ministry.

Even during tough times, Kamiya farmed, his daily routine hardly changing. According to his diary, he continued to grow vegetables such as eggplants, peppers, and squash. Of the others in the colony, more and more were choosing to leave. Oscar Kobayashi had already relocated his family to the Chicago area when Ekiji Shiota returned to Japan in 1925 and Shikazo Ashida moved to California the following year. Also in the 1920s, George Yoshida and his wife, Jean, relocated to another part of

Florida. Jinzo Yamauchi and his wife, Naka, both of whom hailed from the Tango Peninsula, went to Miami in 1928 to engage in landscape gardening. Finally, in the early 1930s, Don Oishi also left to take up residence elsewhere in the state.

In this way, almost all Japanese living in Yamato or nearby departed from the area. Just four households remained: the Kamiya and Hideo Kobayashi families, as well as George Morikami and Shohbi Kamikama. Kamiya, who was the leader of the colony after Jo Sakai's death, had lost his wife. His children had grown to adulthood and, except for his youngest son, Kazuo, left the colony. With the problems he continued to have concerning his farming operation, Kamiya worried about what the future had in store for him. He wrote in his diary on May 18, 1940, an entry with only a few legible passages: "The farmer today is finished. . . . As I wonder what future course I should take . . . I recognize that money is a problem. Settling my debts. . . . Travel expenses to go to Japan." The idea of returning to Japan, then, had entered his mind.

On July 25, 1941, when Japan announced its occupation of French Indochina, the United States froze the assets of Japanese nationals living in the US. This action was part of a wider embargo on exports to Japan. Even Japanese in Florida were unable to withdraw their savings from the banks, and Kamiya could no longer remain at Yamato. He soon left for California, where his eldest daughter, Masa, now lived.

While the Yamato Colony in its early days had a population of around forty individuals year to year, colony members known by name and identified at least once in a written record numbered around seventy. By the time of Kamiya's departure, though, the colony was no longer in existence.

The Buildings of Yamato and US Military Training

On December 7, 1941, Japan launched a surprise attack on Pearl Harbor, Hawai'i, killing more than 2,400 individuals, including civilians, and causing tremendous damage to American battleships and fighter planes. The United States immediately declared war on Japan, and the two countries plunged into all-out war. It was only natural that calls for the expulsion of persons of Japanese ancestry living in the United States quickly became commonplace. With the derogatory term "Jap" in widespread use, stories of attacks on Japanese and Japanese Americans filled the pages of the daily newspapers. Incidents of attacks on Japanese-owned businesses also occurred.

Although the Japanese American community felt nothing but anxiety and bewilderment, society in general held the point of view that persons of Japanese ancestry were likely to cooperate with Japan. Therefore, they must be removed from the West Coast. On February 19, 1942, President Franklin D. Roosevelt signed Executive Order No. 9066 authorizing the United States military to remove or exclude persons of Japanese ancestry from designated military zones at its discretion and without trial.

Military authorities issued a compulsory evacuation order targeting "all persons of Japanese ancestry" living on the West Coast, including first-generation Japanese immigrants as well as second-generation Japanese Americans. Short-term assembly centers that had been set up in eighteen locations, mostly in California, housed 120,000 detainees who fell into these categories. Afterward, these individuals were sent to ten internment camps that had been built in the states of California, Arizona, Wyoming, Utah, Arkansas, and Texas.

Former Yamato resident Oscar Kobayashi and his wife and three children were sent to the Topaz internment camp in the Utah desert as a result of the Japanese removal order. The Kobayashis had been living near San Francisco and had previously resided in the Chicago area following their move from Yamato. Henry Kamiya, who had gone to visit his family in California just before the war, ended up in the Manzanar internment camp in California near the Nevada state line.

Japanese living far from the Pacific coast in Florida were not forced into internment camps like Japanese and Japanese Americans in the states of California, Oregon, and Washington. Nor did these immigrants experience much anti-Japanese hatred. This was probably due to the fact that relatively few Japanese lived in Florida—only 154, according to the 1940 US Census. Yet because they were Japanese and Japanese Americans, they were made to sign a pledge of loyalty. They were treated unfairly and irrationally and even exposed to physical harm. First of all, a 5,820-acre tract of land where the Yamato Colony had been located was confiscated for the establishment of an Army Air Corps technical training base. Later it also became an air base for B-24 bombers. Of the more than 100 individuals owning land in the vicinity of Yamato, fifty non-Japanese families resided within the boundaries of the confiscated land. Even these families had no alternative but to vacate their property.

Remaining in the Yamato area at the beginning of the war were four Japanese households: the family of Hideo Kobayashi, the family of Kazuo Kamiya (third son of Henry Kamiya), George Morikami, and Shohbi Kamikama. While Morikami owned land, he did not live in the affected area but rather in Delray Beach. Kamikama lived nearby the Army Air Force base, just outside of the area that was seized. Neither was affected by the seizure in his day-to-day life to any great extent.

However, the family of Hideo Kobayashi, whose confiscated property included the site of their residence, was affected in a major way. One of the Yamato Colony's early members, Kobayashi came from an isolated backwoods area of Hyōgo Prefecture. In addition, he had created a prosperous life for himself out of nothing. When he first joined the colony, he lived in a tent, then put up a shack in an African American shantytown.

Working with other colonists, Kobayashi planted trees and fruit, dug ditches for irrigation, and expanded the cultivation of fruits and vegetables. He bought a Ford Model A truck, which his wife, Umeko, who was somewhat small in stature, drove in the fields. While she somehow reached the pedals with her feet, the whole family worked together to do the farmwork. In this way their efforts paid off, and soon they built the large American-style house with a porch in which they were living when their property was seized.

However, when farm produce prices dropped nationwide in the 1930s and farming business management became more difficult, Kobayashi made landscaping his livelihood in 1937. He continued to reside in Yamato, making frequent trips back and forth to Ft. Lauderdale, about twenty miles south of his home. His business had most of its clients there. When the time came for Kobayashi and his family to vacate the house, the only compensation they received for it was approximately half of its full market value. Though unhappy with the government, Kobayashi did not know how to challenge it, and he recognized that there was little he could do about his situation.

In the Army Air Force base created on the confiscated land, the house in which both Jo Sakai and Henry Kamiya had once lived remained, along with other buildings appearing just as they always had. With a headline reading, "Florida's Jap Village Only a Memory," an article in the August 6, 1944, issue of the *Miami Herald* describes matter-of-factly how vestiges of the colony, including chicken coops and similar buildings, were treated:

> The barns, sheds, chicken houses and other outbuildings . . . are doing their vital part in preparing young American airmen for combat. Soldiers attacked these buildings with picks, cold chisels and crowbars and now they are twisted piles of wreckage. This wreckage is valuable to the AAF [Army Air Force]. As part of an obstacle course, Yamato's ugly remains are now helping to train Boca Raton field soldiers in the routine of war.

Who Signaled the German U-Boat Lurking Offshore?

Besides having to give up their land, Hideo Kobayashi, George Morikami, and other Japanese had their assets frozen by the government immediately after the beginning of the war. Moreover, Japanese had to obtain permission if they planned to travel anywhere. For Hideo Kobayashi, traveling back and forth to Ft. Lauderdale, where he had clients, could not have been easy. Unless travelers applied for permission, filling in all details on an application—when the trip would occur, where, with whom, for what purpose, and whether they would be meeting someone—the US government prohibited them from making the trip. If a Japanese defied the law, he would be arrested. With this in mind, Kobayashi decided that relocating to Ft. Lauderdale was best, especially after considering how convenient such a move would be to his work.

During the war, the Kobayashis and other Japanese households in southern Florida were watched closely by the authorities. Two Coast Guard servicemen were assigned to live with each household to prevent any possible fifth-column activities from taking place and vouchsafe the safety of the Japanese themselves. In such cases, the Japanese families were required to provide room and board to the Coast Guard personnel, bearing all expenses themselves.

Whenever Kobayashi went out somewhere, one of the young servicemen accompanied him, while the other kept an eye on the Kobayashi residence. One of them was a second-generation German American whose father was living in New York. One day, this young coastguardsman, who was an American citizen, asked Kobayashi's second son, Tamotsu (Tom), a second-generation Japanese American and also an American citizen, "Why am I watching your father like this? No one is keeping an eye on my father in New York."

Tom had no answer, sharing the feeling that the circumstances in which they found themselves were peculiar. But something else was peculiar as well. At about this time, German submarines were attacking and sinking American ships off the coast of Florida. While this was happening, agents of the FBI came to search the Kobayashi house, confiscating a kit from the attic that was used to send messages in Morse code. Tom and his siblings had played with the Morse code kit as children. The coded messages could not be sent over distances greater than a mile, but because it was suspected that someone had been signaling a German U-boat offshore, the agents eyed the kit with suspicion.

The Kobayashis understood clearly the conditions under a state of war, and they knew the position in which they had been placed. Nevertheless, eldest son Theodore Sakaye wanted to enlist in the Army Air Force and serve as a gunner with the crew of a B-17 bomber. Because of an elbow injury, he could not hope to enlist, but his younger brother, Tom, was drafted into the army in 1946 immediately following the war. Tom was dispatched to Okinawa, where he worked with Japanese POWs in protective custody.

As for George Morikami, luckily none of his own property was confiscated. But five days after the attack on Pearl Harbor, the US government took over operation of his farming business, halting the cultivation and marketing of his vegetables. Morikami's assets were frozen while his business was investigated for links to sabotage or other fifth-column activity, a measure that remained in place until the end of January 1942.

In his daily life, Morikami was denied haircuts at the barbershop and refused seeds and fertilizer for growing his crops. When a violent windstorm swept over his farm, it caused considerable damage to his crops. He could not go on by himself. With no other alternatives, Morikami took a job as a tenant farmer on a large farm run by the Macek family, who grew gladioli on a large scale. The Maceks also came under observation during the war years because Morikami worked on their farm. Even so, employment with the Maceks worked out well for Morikami. Although he earned very little, after the war he inherited property from the family. To Morikami, it constituted a substantial fortune.

When Morikami first came to Florida he had no land, and a few years were to pass before he was able to buy any. Some of the land he acquired had been bought from and sold to other members of the Yamato Colony. When he had a little extra money on hand, he bought land and increased his holdings bit by bit. He could not pay large sums at a time, so he bought smaller parcels instead. After the war, he was thus able to repurchase some of the land that he had sold off before the financial panic of 1929.

Homesick

Farming among Resort Communities

After the war, new roads were built in southern Florida, vehicles increased in number, and urban areas underwent change. In the town of Palm Beach, the site of Henry Flagler's former residence, Worth Avenue was no longer an uneven dirt road, but was lined with exclusive shops selling quality brand-name merchandise. Beneath the palm trees planted along the town's streets, automobiles lined up in formation. Flashy wide-bodied Cadillacs, Chryslers, and Fords showed off the signature look of the era with tailfins thrusting outward like wings, mimicking the appearance of jet planes.

Even in the towns of Delray Beach and Boca Raton the number of autos had increased, palm trees lined the shore, and beach resorts had been developed. Lifeguard stations stood on the beach. Collapsible dome-shaped sunshades were made available for rent, and during tourist season the entire beach was filled with them, like so many hermit crabs.

Crowds of seasonal tourists from northern states could be seen along Florida's famous beaches, where boardwalks had been installed and beachside restaurants were popular. At the rocky outcropping today called Yamato Rock, the shadows of the Japanese settlers were no longer visible on the sand, and the once wild, undeveloped land that they had known had given way to resort towns and residential neighborhoods. For many, Florida after the war was like a vision of paradise—a glorious dream come true—everywhere up and down the coast.

Away from the bothersome annoyance of the growth that was taking place, Morikami continued to farm his land as he always had. He drew a line that he did not cross at development, and he lived a simple life close to nature. He raised vegetables and pineapples, occasionally bought property, and, when he saw the opportunity, sold property. Morikami, who had no family of his own, spent his free time avidly reading.

With an active love of learning, Morikami had an interest in world affairs and enjoyed reading books and monthly magazines like *Kingu* (King), which he had sent to him from Japan. He even subscribed to the newspaper from his hometown of Miyazu. In addition, he eagerly researched farming practices and techniques by reading books for a thorough understanding of the subjects. From Japan, he ordered seeds for several varieties of vegetables and other plants, experimenting with them in his fields.

After the war, the only two former settlers of the colony who continued to farm land they owned near the colony site were Morikami and Shohbi Kamikama. Kamikama was born in 1889, the fourth son in a farming household located in the seaside community of Kominato (today part of Minami Satsuma City) on the Satsuma Peninsula of Kagoshima Prefecture. He seems to have been an eager student who completed his education through middle school, according to the old system (the prefectural middle school from which he graduated is today Kawanabe High School). Kamikama traveled to the US at the age of eighteen. In order to fund his passage, his family members mortgaged some of their landholdings. While his passport application stated that his purpose for entering the US was language study, after arriving he procured work instead.

From Seattle, where he had disembarked, Kamikama made his way to New York and found employment as a waiter. Unable to endure the cold of winter, he relocated to Florida in 1917, taking up farming in Yamato eleven years after Morikami's own arrival. Kamikama had almost no farming experience. He lived a frugal lifestyle and, like Morikami, invested in land. Known for his temperamental disposition, he did not get along well with Morikami even though both men were Japanese.

Avidly Writing Letters to Japan

Morikami's father, Takezō Morigami (to use the preferred spelling of the family name after Morikami's departure), died in 1934 at the age of seventy; his mother, Soyo, passed away at age eighty-one just before the end of the war. Morikami did not return home either time. Six children were born to the Morigami household: four boys, of whom Sukeji was the eldest, and two girls. One son and one daughter, the last child born, died in infancy. Of the four remaining children, Sukeji went to America, followed by younger brother Masabei, who also joined the Yamato Colony but soon returned home to Miyazu. Youngest son Yoneji left the Morigami household as the adopted son of another family, the Okamotos. Sukeji's younger sister Fude married Motoji Ida, taking her husband's name but continuing to live in the Morigami house. Brother-in-law Motoji was angry with Morikami because he never came home to pay his respects at his parents' gravesite despite being their eldest son.

Morikami never once returned to Japan. Nevertheless he worried about the family's affairs and the future of the household. He wrote letters to his sister Fude frequently. Because he was so far away, Morikami told his siblings, it would not be his place to intervene if problems were to arise concerning inheritance of the house or other assets. He told them that he hoped they would amicably settle whatever differences they might have.

Morikami often exchanged letters with the family of his brother Yoneji. This was probably because of Yoneji's accidental death in November 1943. During the war, Yoneji was employed at a munitions plant in Amagasaki, Japan, near Osaka. He is said to have died in a fall from a building, but it is also claimed that he was thrown from the building while in police custody because of his antiwar beliefs.

Born in 1900, Yoneji married Mitsue Okamoto and entered the Okamoto family as an adopted heir. The couple had two sons and two daughters, with eldest son Osamu followed by eldest daughter Reiko, second son Mikio, and second daughter Akiko. When Yoneji died at age forty-two, Osamu was thirteen years old, while Akiko was only two.

At the end of the war, Morikami was deeply saddened to learn of Yoneji's death. He recalled Yoneji on the morning he had left home so many years before. Little more than a toddler, Yoneji had clung to him and wept, "I want to go, too!" Morikami was also deeply concerned about the welfare of his sister-in-law, the widow Yoneji had left behind, and her family, so he began writing to her around 1950. At the same time, he began sending money from America to assist with their daily living expenses.

A prolific correspondent, Morikami sent letters addressed to the Okamotos several times a month. He told them the circumstances of his life: about his health, about his farming income, about storm damage to his crops, about his plans, his personal assets, and buying and selling real estate.

Memories of his hometown and reminiscences of the past appeared any number of times in his letters. Morikami had completed his education only through primary school and had worked on the family farm, but he was well read. He often dropped quotations from the classics and other works of literature into his writing. Having been born near the end of the nineteenth century during Japan's Meiji Period, Morikami used quite a few antiquated Sino-Japanese characters in his correspondence. By contrast, having been in the United States for a long period of time, he also liberally sprinkled in words from English, which he wrote in *katakana*, a syllabary used for writing foreign words in Japanese. He used characters in a simplified form in which one seemed to flow into another, making them difficult to decipher in only one reading. Writing in columns, Morikami completely filled up both sides of the thin-paper aerograms.

In his letters, Morikami always addressed his sister-in-law Mitsue familiarly as either Mi-chan or Mi-san. In a letter dated May 1950, he opened his heart to her and told her what his life was like:

Today I was busy all day working with three African Americans to harvest my eggplants. I shipped close to 100 crates (around 4,620 lbs.) by train and by truck to markets in the north. Market prices are not very favorable, but . . . I should get 75¢ to the pound for them.

It's like summer here in Florida. Indoors, the temperature is nearly 90° Fahrenheit, but at night it drops down to around 75°. The humidity is high, but this is not the same kind of heat that is experienced in the rest of the country, since cool breezes blow off of the Atlantic Ocean day and night. Like other people, I work all day long almost naked, not even wearing a hat.

Because I don't speak or write in Japanese for long periods of time, I find it difficult writing letters. . . . Since I will have some spare time in a couple of weeks, I will tell you all of my secrets then even if it means confessing my entire life.

Already this year it is May. On May 4, 1906, I arrived here at 9:15 in the evening after traveling alone for 8,000 miles. When I reflect on those days, I can't help but be overcome with emotion.

Again there is trouble in the world. Many in the United States are alarmed that war is imminent. I am worried about what will happen to Japan should World War III break out. I wonder if I can bring all of you to the U.S. [as Japan is not a safe place]. It won't be very long until we Japanese living in the United States will be granted the right to become American citizens. If this happens, bringing you here should be much easier.

"Mi-san, on the 24th I sent only $100 to assist you," Morikami had written to his sister-in-law in a previous letter. "I live in a hovel with a leaking roof; I ride in a rattle-trap of a car; I don't have a radio, but read the newspaper and magazines by the light of a dim oil lamp. After a hard day, going to sleep is what I most look forward to."

At this time in his life, Morikami operated a farm that was about five miles from downtown Delray Beach. He hired African American farmhands and worked in his fields while pondering the time that had passed since he had come to the United States over forty-five years earlier. He went around stripped to the waist under the intense heat of the May sun. Morikami also drove an automobile that rattled, and after dark he made do with a lamp that did not use electricity. Moreover, his modest home leaked whenever it rained. This was the life he described in his correspondence, which continued to reveal personal details.

Some of the correspondence that George Morikami sent to the Okamoto family in the 1950s (photo by Ryusuke Kawai).

For example, in 1952 Morkami wrote about seeing the Japanese film *Rashomon*, directed by Akira Kurosawa, when it played in Miami. By the summer of 1953 he noted that the cultivation of vegetables in his fields was his only source of income, forcing him into debt. In addition, Morikami described reading an article in the Japanese journal *Kingu* about the pardon of Japanese war criminals by Filipino president Elpidio Quirino. It moved him to tears.

Finally, recollecting his days of farming in Miyazu, Morikami thought wistfully of the woven straw hats that farmers used to wear in summer. He contacted family members in Miyazu to try to get one sent to him. Though it was just a short drive for him to go from his farm into town, where people had electricity, Morikami liked his simple, primitive lifestyle. Five cats were his companions in an unassuming residence on the outskirts of town.

Becoming Uncle Long-Legs

Morikami reached his sixtieth birthday soon after the war ended. He seemed to be growing ever fonder of what he called his "family." As he exchanged letters with them and provided financial assistance, his relationship with his sister-in-law Mitsue and with her children became very much like that between husband and wife and parent and child.

As an uncle, Morikami offered his nieces and nephews advice on education, manners, employment, and marriage, sometimes arguing with Mitsue via correspondence. While discussing family matters, Morikami and Mitsue even considered marriage to one another. If he sold his property, Morikami reasoned, he could return to Japan where they could live together as a family. Or, if that would not do, he could become a US citizen and have Mitsue come join him in America.

In a letter, Osamu called Morikami, whom he had never met, "Father." To this Morikami replied, "To be called Father for the first time in my life makes me so happy. . . . It's a feeling I cannot put into words." To Mitsue, though, he said, "He should call me his American uncle." While Morikami, Osamu, and Mitsue had different issues and circumstances to think about as they considered the future, communication was made all the more difficult by the distance between them. As a result, their feelings about the options open to them swung one way, then the other.

Occasionally Morikami gave the Okamoto children gifts, such as the baseball gloves he sent to Osamu and Mikio. Coaxing him, Reiko told Morikami what she wanted, including items like writing materials. Presents arrived for Akiko, who was several years younger than the other children, even without her asking for them. When she was in her fourth year of elementary school, Morikami sent her a pair of white leather boots. Akiko was deeply moved by the gift because she had never seen anything like them in Japan.

As for expenses related to the children's educations, Morikami paid everything. When Akiko, who said that she wanted to go to junior college, sent him her grades, he wrote back, "You should not worry about school expenses. From now on, I will take responsibility for them. I will be responsible for all of your expenses while you are enrolled in school. Make me a chart for your yearly school tuition and all of your other expenses and send it to me right away." The children called this big-hearted uncle Ashinaga Oji-san, or "Uncle Long-Legs," after the novel *Daddy-Long-Legs*, about an orphaned girl with a secret benefactor.

Sadly, in September 1953, twenty-four-year-old Osamu died of illness. In a letter to Mitsue, Morikami wrote, "There are no words I can say that will comfort you. I wept [at the news]. Our loved ones, Yoneji and Osamu, both gone." His grief was palpable.

Morikami worried about the smallest details of the children's lives. He was concerned about the kind of instruction Akiko, who was learning English, was receiving in high school. Thus he wrote a letter to her English instructor, asking the teacher, "Please take care of my niece." Again, Morikami did not just provide Akiko with money to cover her school expenses. He asked for an itemized breakdown of how she was spending it. Even about the postage for sending a letter Morikami told his niece, "Your letters are always short, so there is no need to send them by regular airmail ([which costs] 70-sen). A 45-sen aerogram is sufficient." He even gave advice on economizing on such items as envelopes.

Morikami also gave his opinion on the behavior of women. Once, he learned that Reiko was going to Tōkyō to meet an American man who was an acquaintance. "You should be ashamed," he scolded her. "I have heard that Japanese morals have broken down completely." Morikami had seen pictures of young Japanese women in the company of American soldiers who were in Japan as part of the Allied occupation. To him, the behavior of the women seemed indiscreet. Because he felt this way, he was critical of Reiko's easygoing relationship with the American.

One night during that same year, Morikami was attacked by a burglar after he had gone to bed. His residence was more than a 100 yards away from his nearest neighbor, and he did not have a telephone. He sustained serious injury to his head and other areas of his body. Fortunately, an acquaintance happened to visit him the next day, enabling him to get medical treatment at a hospital. The incident was an opportunity for Morikami to acquire a handgun to use for self-protection, which the police recommended.

In June of 1955, Morikami purchased a small trailer in which to live. This residence could be used by only a couple of people, and he could move easily by towing it with his car. In addition, it had a kitchen, a toilet, and a shower, as well as other features. Although the trailer was new, Morikami's daily routine was not. He awoke around five o'clock every morning and returned from the fields every evening after seven. His stomach would be empty, but he would be too tired to do anything about it. Instead, he would end up falling asleep on the couch with his shoes on, just as he always had.

From this time Morikami's physical condition began troubling him more and more. He suffered from a chronic hernia. On top of that, he lost almost all of his teeth. The treatment he sought to prevent his gums from rubbing against each other made his face swell like a balloon. Furthermore, the aftereffects of stomach ulcers occasionally bothered him, causing him to spit up large quantities of blood. Worried about the possibility of cancer, Morikami wrote to Mitsue, "I want to re-write my will."

A Desire to Leave His Name on the Land

"I've Been Here Since the Meiji Period"

A who's who of Japanese residing in the US titled *Nichibei Jūsho Roku* (Japanese American Address Directory), published in San Francisco in 1939, listed twenty-three Japanese living in Florida just before the beginning of World War II. While the number of Japanese increased in growing cities like Miami and St. Petersburg in the years following the war, to encounter a Japanese in rural Florida where Morikami lived was rare.

One morning in September 1956, Morikami left home for the Delray Beach post office. Morikami, who to that time had lived in a modest shack before moving to a trailer, conducted business through the mail, and he checked his post-office box daily to see what mail he had received. As the elderly farmer finished up his business and walked out of the one-story post office building on this particular day, he saw a young man who appeared to be Japanese standing in the parking lot. The man's back was turned toward Morikami.

"*Anata Nihonjin desu ka?* [Are you a Japanese?]," Morikami called out in a loud voice.

The young man quickly turned in the direction of Morikami's voice, surprised to hear his own language being spoken. Standing before him was a short-statured elderly man whom he took to be another Japanese. The man was dressed in a shirt and trousers that looked like work clothes, while a big smile spread across his broad face.

"I never thought that I would meet a Japanese in such a place," the surprised youth, whose name was Shunji (James) Mihori, said later. Mihori was planning to move to Delray Beach from Miami, where he had been a postgraduate student at the University of Miami. Although he had yet to graduate, he had recently found a job in Delray. He was at the Delray post office to give notice of his change of address.

As Mihori stood beside his wood-paneled Ford Galaxy station wagon, Morikami asked him, "When did you get here?"

"I came just yesterday," Mihori replied.

With a grin, the elderly farmer told him, "I've been here since the Meiji Period."

Mihori was astonished. How could a Japanese have been in such an out-of-the-way place since as long ago as the Meiji Period, he wondered. Morikami told him about the Yamato Colony.

Japanese Wanted

The story of how Morikami, who had been born in Meiji Period Japan, happened to be living in Delray Beach was indeed surprising, but no more so than Mihori's own story. Working toward a postgraduate degree in advertising, the student was in the habit of perusing the newspaper daily. One day, as he scanned the *Miami Herald* as usual, he ran across a help-wanted ad that read, "Japanese Wanted." The advertisement had been posted by an American company that simply sought a Japanese, and not to work as an interpreter or in a restaurant. When he saw the same ad again the following day, Mihori's interest was aroused.

Seeking to hire a Japanese was Warren G. Grimes, president of the Grimes Manufacturing Company. Headquartered in Ohio, the firm manufactured lighting systems for airplanes; during World War II it was said that all American military planes were equipped with lighting systems produced by Grimes's company.

Raised in an orphanage after the death of his father, Grimes completed his education only through the fifth grade. Despite these hardships, though, he built a successful company and was recognized as an entrepreneur and inventor who was called the "father of the aircraft lighting industry."

Although the company's head office was in Ohio, after the war Grimes spent winters in the warm climate of Florida for reasons of health. He built a winter residence in Ft. Lauderdale and, later, another one in Delray Beach. In 1957 he established a center for research and development near his residence in Delray and did much of his work there. In seeking to hire a Japanese, and only a Japanese, Grimes wanted someone to work alongside him as a personal attendant and consultant.

There was a reason for this. A childhood friend of Grimes's was Gen. Robert Eichelberger, commanding officer of the Eighth US Army in the Pacific Theater during World War II. Second only to Gen. Douglas McArthur in command of the US Army, this famous general supervised troops at Leyte and other battles in the Philippines. At the cessation of hostilities, he established command headquarters in Yokohama for the Allied occupation of Japan.

Repeatedly in the midst of battle with the Japanese army, Eichelberger was conscious of the strength and determination of the Japanese. Even though they were the enemy when he formed his opinion of their abilities, he advised his friend Warren Grimes, "If you hire anyone, hire a Japanese." Grimes had never met anyone from Japan, but he trusted Eichelberger's advice—hence the recruitment effort through the "Japanese Wanted" ad in the newspaper.

Born in Kamakura in 1933, Mihori was a graduate of the Economics Department of Gakushuin University. He joined a *kabuki* study group during his university days, and he was employed as a student *kabuki* actor. For a time he considered making acting in traditional theater his career. Just before graduation, though, he was injured when a stage prop fell and hit him on the back of the head. Because of the incident he decided against pursuing *kabuki* further.

Mihori, who had always had an interest in American film and stage musicals, took lessons in American conversational English while at the university. His English-language instructor was a young American who had graduated from Stanford University. This teacher completely changed the way Mihori regarded the study of English from something that he initially detested to something that held his interest. Mihori therefore resolved to study abroad in the United States.

Mihori sought a location to complete his studies that was unlikely to attract other Japanese, resulting in his decision in favor of Miami. As he expected, there were just a few Japanese in the Florida city. For that matter, when Mihori entered graduate school at the University of Miami, there were no students at all from anywhere in East Asia. Because of this, when he saw the "Japanese Wanted" ad, he thought, "Probably no one but me is likely to read this. It must be fate." With such thoughts in mind, he responded to the post-office box number published in the ad.

Grimes interviewed Mihori, determined that the young man satisfied his expectations, and hired him. Mihori moved into the Grimes residence in Delray Beach before completing his studies at the University of Miami. Commuting back and forth to grad school, he worked for Grimes when he wasn't attending classes.

When Mihori first began his study abroad he intended to return to Japan. He promised Chieko, his fiancée who was one of the younger students in the *kabuki* study group, that he would be back in one year. But continuing his employment with Grimes was a tremendous opportunity for Mihori, and he decided against returning to Japan. Instead, Chieko traveled to the US in 1953 to make a home for the two of them in Florida.

Surprised by the chance meeting with this Japanese named George Morikami, Mihori asked him after a moment, "Would you be interested in meeting my boss?" Grimes was a self-made industrialist who had built a major manufacturing firm in one generation. With a dislike for people with only a college education to boast of, he was fond of making statements such as "I hate college kids." Morikami was the "Old Man of Meiji" who struggled tremendously in rural southern Florida with no one to rely on but himself. Mihori had a feeling that something would click between the two of them.

With Mihori's station wagon in the lead and Morikami following in his pickup truck, they paid a visit to Warren Grimes. Grimes and

Morikami hit it off, with the result that Mihori and Grimes began to spend time with the elderly farmer now and then. Grimes would have lighthearted discussions with Morikami and call him George.

Around this time Morikami lost nearly all of his teeth. One evening, Mihori's wife, Chieko, invited Morikami to the couple's home to treat him to dinner, but Morikami hardly touched his food the entire evening. Chieko wondered at first whether Morikami was being modest. However, she soon realized that since he had almost no teeth he was unable to eat food that had not been specially prepared. She thought that if he had told her, she could have accommodated his needs. Chieko understood, though, that his pride had prevented him from saying anything.

Concerned for Morikami's welfare, Grimes said to him, "George, why don't you go see a dentist? I'll introduce you to one I know." To which Morikami replied, "I will take care of this one way or another myself." Ever stubborn, Morikami would not listen to the advice of others.

On another occasion, Morikami mentioned that he had never once returned to Japan. "George, why don't you go?" Grimes asked. "If it's a question of money, I'll give you some." He pulled a wad of dollar bills from his pocket. Grimes always walked around with thousands of dollars in ready cash. When he was young he had lived in poverty, and because of that, he felt uneasy if he didn't have cash on hand. Even this offer Morikami declined.

At the time Morikami owned quite a bit of land, but unlike Grimes he did not have much ready cash. Land that he probably would have sold he could not, so he managed somehow on revenue from his vegetable fields. A few years previously he had suffered from a serious illness and had nothing with which to pay his hospital bill. Morikami had worked in the hospital's vegetable garden and pawned his farming tools, applying whatever he earned toward what he owed the hospital. And although he had no material possessions to speak of, he still had taxes to pay on his land. Eventually, Morikami would come to rely on Mihori's expertise in American law to decide what to do in the future with the land that he owned.

To Go to Japan or To Go to South America?

Perhaps because his connection with Japan deepened through his correspondence with the Okamoto family, Morikami's feelings of homesickness became even stronger around 1960. Such feelings, though, were complex, as was apparent in his letters to Japan. "While it's unlikely that I'll give a second thought to ever returning to Japan, which I feel I don't want to do, my thoughts return unconsciously to my hometown," he wrote in June 1953. Because a neighbor of his in Florida acted with kindness toward him, he wrote in July 1958, "My feelings of homesickness fade away day by day."

For every time Morikami thought he would tell the Okamotos, "After serious consideration, I've decided to apply for American citizenship," he would also propose returning to Japan and building a house in which to live in the Kyōto suburbs. Based on experience, Morikami knew that building an affordable home in Florida was possible, even if the cost included a 250-acre lot. But he also knew that the price of land in Japan was terribly high, and he was discouraged that he could not possibly afford to build a home there.

After awhile, Morikami began to consider that maybe his destiny lay in South America. "What I want is something like a civilized country but without any of the world's big cities, a country that is partly developed, even backward. The ruins of the Incan empire, 8,000 feet up in the Andes Mountains of South America, the great rain forest unexplored at the upper reaches of the Amazon River. I wonder if I would be healthy enough to realize my dream [to go there]," he wrote the Okamotos in December 1958.

At the beginning of 1959 Morikami told the Okamotos, "Once the harvest is in, I will definitely go to South America." In June of the same year, he stated firmly, "In one month, I am going." In the end, Morikami never realized his plan, although even a year later he wrote to his sister Fude, "I will go to South America for as long as a year to look over the situation there. Then, if I come back here [to Florida], I will make a visit to Japan."

Whenever Morikami seriously considered returning to Japan, his feelings of homesickness intensified. At the same time, his spirits were buoyed by thoughts of travel to South America. Morikami had heard comments by Japanese who had immigrated to the US before the war and later had gone to South America. He also had read reports from Japan. From these current reports he knew that Japanese immigration to South America had resumed after the war. He himself had considered immigrating there—like Seitō Saibara had done, going to Brazil from Texas and establishing a plantation there. It was a plan to which Morikami gave serious thought. On the one hand, land was less expensive in South America than it was in Florida—where rural areas were gradually but inevitably giving way to urbanization anyway. Also, farming in South America was possible on a large scale. On the other hand, Morikami probably would feel homesick for Florida there, too.

Then again, an acquaintance of his had bought and cleared considerable acreage in Honduras and had invited Morikami to join him. If he were younger, and if he had a son, he could follow his dream of starting over in South America. He became excited just thinking about it. Morikami expressed his thoughts in a letter that was an earnest appeal to his niece Reiko. "Sometimes I wish you were a boy," he wrote. He continued as follows:

> You are liberal-minded and daring. You are honest and have a strong sense of responsibility. You would probably fulfill my dream perfectly, I am certain. I still have 190 acres of land. If I were to sell it, it would be worth forty times what land is worth in South America. With the money from the sale I would be able to buy 7,600 acres for the same amount. Clearing the land little by little each year, I would plant tropical fruit such as banana, pineapple and coconut, and also raise cattle. In a few years my farm would yield a crop. But it would be a very difficult undertaking. To young people these days who only talk, who aren't fit and who lack nerve, such a dream would be out of reach.

Morikami also knew something about Japanese immigrants to the Dominican Republic in the Caribbean. In May 1962, he wrote a letter to the Consulate General of Japan in New Orleans. He wanted to send some Japanese magazines and other things he had to the Dominican Republic and asked how he should go about doing it. In response to this, Consul General Shinjiro Wakayama asked him if the items could be presented through the Japanese embassy in the Dominican Republic.

Morikami wrote to the Japanese embassy there, after which he received a polite letter in reply: "Please contact the Immigration Affairs Bureau, Santo Domingo Branch, which is the office that assists immigrants. They will be happy to circulate the materials you wish to donate to Japanese living here."

A Never-Ending Yearning for His First Love

Morikami often thought about old age and, along with it, his boyhood home. He reminisced about his childhood in letters. Morikami described the persimmon and cypress and other fruit trees that had been planted at his old house since he had been away. He also remembered the beautiful peaches like those he had drawn pictures of as a child, when he had been warned, "If you touch them, they will spoil." Morikami had waited until the peaches ripened to eat them, although his mother had taken the best ones to the store to sell.

Morikami's favorite grandfather had been a courier for the Miyazu Domain during the feudal period, covering the circuit between Kyōto and Edo. He had told his grandson marvelous tales of the fifty-three stations along the Tōkaidō Road, and he had picked up sticks of ink here and there for the youngster who liked to draw. Morikami's grandmother was a kindly person who was short in stature. Such reminiscences he recorded in letters largely in order to comfort himself.

A letter that he wrote one night mentioned his younger brother Tokuji, who had died in infancy. Worried about a powerful hurricane that was approaching, Morikami was unable to sleep. "When I am lying awake worrying about one thing or another, thoughts of long ago sometimes come to mind," he wrote to the Okamotos.

A few nights ago I recollected things that had happened when I was a young child. You probably don't know it, but I used to have another brother. His name was Tokuji. He was about two years younger than me. As a baby, he was well-behaved, and almost never cried.

When I would stab a steamed dumpling with a chopstick for him, he would take it in both hands and eat it happily with his *miso-shiru* soup, chortling with delight. He died of measles (probably fever) about the time he was three. I remember my mother crying on top of his tiny coffin. His gravestone was in the northwest corner of the family grave plot. It was an oval, gray, natural stone about a foot and a half tall. Tokuji's posthumous name that is carved on it includes the word "*dōji*" [child], but other than that I don't remember clearly how it read.

Morikami's feelings of nostalgia for his hometown were reflected in his charitable giving to Miyazu, too. Shortly after the war, his brother Masabei appealed to the people of Miyazu to fund the installation of a stone monument memorializing those who had lost their lives in the war. Masabei asked Morikami whether he wanted to contribute to the project as well.

The monument, which resembles a large stone cube, was installed in 1959 in a park overlooking the city. Standing nearby is a stone lantern around ten feet in height, funded by Morikami's gift. Carved on it in large characters is the inscription, "Beikoku Morikami Sukeji [Sukeji Morikami, United States]."

Moreover, in 1960, when Masabei informed him that an elementary school in Miyazu was to be rebuilt, Morikami donated $500 toward the project. He donated to a kindergarten in the area as well.

Morikami got it into his head that it was somehow possible to transcend the boundaries of time and space and reconnect with Hatsu (in letters he wrote her name as Hatsuko), the love he had left behind in his hometown. She remained only as a fleeting memory to him.

For the first time in twenty years, Morikami exchanged letters with his younger brother Masabei, who had stopped writing to him after the death of their father in 1934. "When you grow old, you miss the town where you spent your childhood," Morikami wrote in a letter to Masabei. "You get sick, you can't sleep at night, etc. You don't know what to think any more. Your mind runs back to the hometown you no longer know." In the same letter, a few lines later, Morikami suddenly asked about the girl who was his first love, Hatsu Onizawa. Perhaps because he had spent so much time in America, he got straight to the point where his emotions were concerned.

"What I want to ask you is about Hatsuko Onizawa," he wrote. "She was the older sister of Jūtarō, whom you know. She was my first love.

You must not laugh at my foolishness, and you must not tell anyone. From time to time I see her in my dreams. She looks exactly like she did the day we said our final good-byes. Now I only want to wish her good health and much happiness."

Morikami also wrote a letter to Hatsu. Since he did not know her current family name because of her marriage, and he did not know where she lived, he decided to send the letter to her through Masabei. He asked his brother to look up Hatsu's address and deliver it for him.

Morikami's sister Fude happened to be at Masabei's house when the letter arrived, so Masabei asked her to deliver it. Fude then visited the house where Hatsu lived, but she did not find her at home. According to Fude, she gave the letter addressed to Hatsu to a boy who was looking after the house while the owners were away.

It is certain that the letter got to the house, but whether it was ever placed in Hatsu's hands is unknown. Perhaps she had read the letter but could not correctly address an envelope to Morikami's home in America to send a reply. After all, it was unlikely that she was able to write using the English alphabet. Whatever the reason, Morikami never received an answer from Hatsu. Turning over in his mind one explanation after another, he just became more and more distraught.

Writing to Fude, Morikami double-checked that his letter had indeed been delivered. It was the autumn of 1960. Hurricane Donna, which caused tremendous damage on the East Coast of the United States, had just struck Florida. Immediately afterward, Morikami reported in his letter to Fude, "We were struck by Typhoon Donna packing winds of 150 miles per hour. It churned violently up the Atlantic coast 2000 miles from the southern tip of Florida northeast as far as Boston. Thankfully, because 100 miles separated Delray from the eye of the storm, we escaped damage, but I had to stay alert, hardly getting any sleep, for two days and two nights." He added what sounded like a proverb: "Natural disasters are like life; neither hardships nor blessings last forever."

Abrubtly Morikami switched to the subject of Hatsu. "I'm a little concerned about my letter to Hatsuko," he wrote.

The contents, as you know, I don't want anyone to know about. I don't know who the child was that you gave the letter to. Is the letter now in the hands of that child's family? Is it being kept safe?

Has it been thrown away? Although it's probably a lot of trouble for you, I want to ask you to go to the child's family for me and ask them to tell you what happened to it, fully and clearly. If it hasn't already been thrown away, if by chance nothing has happened to it, have the letter returned to you and mail it to Hatsuko for me, I beg you again and again.

By this time, Morikami was seventy-three years old. Lacking information regarding the fate of the letter to Hatsu, he expressed his frustrations even to his nieces in the Okamoto family. "The fate of the letter to Hatsuko-san is troubling to me," he wrote. "Did it arrive? Did it not arrive? There is no way of knowing."

Morikami's sister-in-law Mitsue was also aware of the missing letter. Without telling him, she looked into the matter herself. She found Hatsu's residence, thinking she had done well. When Morikami found out that she had gone to see Hatsu, though, he blew the matter out of all proportion. Discovering that his letter had never reached Hatsu, he expressed his irritation. "With this I have completely lost my dignity," he told Mitsue, adding, "But I still have hope. This is a once-in-a-lifetime love." Morikami continued, "Anybody can have secrets. My secrets are like those of other people; they must be protected. My secrets were exposed pitifully for everyone to see. Hereafter, in all matters like this I want you to keep your mouth shut. That would be best."

In correspondence to his niece Akiko, Morikami wrote about his deep affection for Hatsu in the bitter, painful days he experienced when he first came to Florida. He closed the letter by asking Akiko's advice.

I had found a job clearing land at a place 180 miles north of Yamato through advertising in the newspaper. The job was on about ten acres working by myself as hard as I could while living in a shack out in the middle of nowhere, for only about a dollar per day. . . . A letter came from Japan. It was the news that Hatsuko-san had gotten married. Hatsuko, whom I missed dearly, had forsaken me forever. I was shocked, stunned; there was nothing I could do but cry. I gave up on any idea of returning to Japan, and severed all connections with my hometown. Since then, for over fifty years, my dreams of Hatsuko-san have never faded. Even a few nights ago, I dreamed I returned to Japan. As I dropped off to sleep in a hotel room, I could hear coming from the next room the voices of two women, who seemed to be a mother and her daughter, talking. I listened intently. Without a doubt the daughter's voice was Hatsuko-san's! Suddenly, poof! The dream ended, cruelly for me. Now, Hatsu is a seventy-year-old woman.

The Hatsuko that I see in my dreams is always the sweet girl of my youth. Now she is living in Kyōto. She never received the letter that your aunt was supposed to deliver. Should I keep Hatsuko secretly in my heart just as she is in my dreams? Or should I go back to Japan and see her again? I can't make a decision. Akiko, what would you do?

Even though many decades had passed, Hatsu still appeared in Morikami's dreams. By the time he wrote to Akiko, he had found out that Hatsu was living in Kyōto, and he knew the address. Hoping to see her again, Morikami began to consider a trip back to Japan, although he had been away more than half a century. In the summer of 1960, he inquired by letter to the Consulate General of Japan in New Orleans about the necessary procedures for the trip, including the matter of a passport. He soon received an answer. Morikami was told that he must be issued a new passport if the one in his possession was from before the war and had "Dai Nihon Teikoku [Imperial Japan]" printed on it.

Right away he sent the consulate the passport that had been issued to him in 1906. He also submitted an application with his photograph and the handling fee attached to it. Thus, Morikami obtained a new passport allowing him to return to Japan whenever he wanted.

The Dream of a Morikami Agriculture Experimental Station

Should he return to Japan, go to South America, or remain in the United States? His emotions were in turmoil, but still Morikami faced the daily necessity of tending to his crops. Through the Okamoto family he had ordered seeds from Japan and was now growing plants from them. These were experimental efforts, as if his farm were the "Morikami Agriculture Experimental Station," as he called it. Because the cherry tree seeds he had obtained originally did not grow, he tried again with the varieties called *yama-zakura* (mountain-cherry) and *botan-zakura* (peony-cherry, so named because its blossoms have multiple layers of petals). Pine, maple, tea—one by one he planted them as well as others. He moved forward with his life, engaging in such projects on his own while reciting lines from his favorite Chinese poem:

薄命よく伸ぶ旬日の寿

Hakumei yoku nobu junjitsu no kotobuki

Sadly, beauty lasts but a short duration.

In addition, Morikami proposed to begin developing his 190 acres of property over a five-year period during which he intended to create a pond and a hill and plant fruit and other trees.

Morikami planned first to dig a well on the property and build a storage shed for farm tools and machinery. He then planned to put in a one-and-a-half-acre pond and stock it with *koi* (Japanese ornamental carp) and other fish. On one side of the pond he planned to build a residence combining architectural elements from both East and West, and on the other side he planned to create a miniature replica of Mt. Fuji that would rise to a height of a hundred feet. At its foot, Morikami's design called for young pines to be planted along the edge of the pond, like the ancient pines at Miho no Matsubara in Shizuoka Prefecture, Japan. He also planned a bridge in imitation of one that spans the southern end of Lake Biwa at Ōtsu in Shiga Prefecture.

Morikami planned to leave a hundred acres of his property untouched as a pine forest. On the remainder of the land, he intended to create a nursery and a laboratory for different varieties of vegetables and flowering plants. As magnificent as the plan was, though, he had no one on whom to rely to help him see it through.

While the pond was being excavated, Morikami fell and broke a rib. He was also involved in an automobile accident and had his driver's license revoked. Moreover, he was constantly suffering pain in his leg joints and hands due to arthritis, and his intestines were blocked and he was unable to eat, perhaps from the aftereffects of surgery he had once had for stomach ulcers. For nourishment, Morikami took to sucking food through a tube. Though his pain was so excruciating he thought he would die, the work continued little by little despite his ill health.

Then, on July 24, 1962, former Yamato colonist Jinzo Yamauchi and his wife, Naka, who had moved to Miami some years before, died in an automobile accident when their car was struck by a train at a railroad crossing. Two others, Kayo Tashiro, wife of Miami Beach developer Shigezo Tashiro, and Miami resident Teiji Nakamura, were also riding in the vehicle. They were on their way home after attending a going-away party for Giichi Yamada, the proprietor of a food distribution company in Miami who was returning to Japan. All four passengers were killed. Morikami had also intended to ride with them that evening, but urgent business detained him, and he escaped the fate of the others.

Yamauchi hailed from the Tango Peninsula. Once during the previous year, Morikami had spent the night at the Yamauchi residence. As their conversation had become more animated, Yamauchi had divulged that he would soon return to Japan to live either in his hometown of Mineyama or in Miyazu. Beginning with colony leader Jo Sakai, many of Morikami's fellow countrymen had come from the Tango Peninsula as pioneers to Florida. Now, with Yamauchi's death, Morikami was the last of them to remain.

In Kyōto that same year, the life of Henry Kamiya, who had been the central figure in the colony following the death of Jo Sakai, came to an end at the age of eighty-seven years. Kamiya had been interned in California during the war after moving there shortly before the commencement of hostilities. He had returned to Florida for a time after the war ended. After spending additional time in California, he had eventually returned to Japan, building a house in Kyōto where he lived out the remainder of his life. In West Palm Beach, Kamiya's name was engraved on his wife's gravestone.

Wanting to Adopt

The interest in America shown by the Okamotos' eldest daughter, Reiko, and second son, Mikio, grew as they exchanged correspondence with Morikami. Both even tackled the study of English. For Morikami's part, the idea formed in the mind of this unmarried man to adopt his niece Reiko. For this reason he began to consider seeking naturalization, since he believed the adoption process would be easier for him if he were to acquire American citizenship.

Morikami consulted with Mihori about adopting Reiko. In the summer of 1963, Mr. and Mrs. Mihori were planning a visit to Japan. Morikami asked them to meet with Mitsue, his sister-in-law and Reiko's mother, to let her know of his hope to bring his niece to the United States as his adopted daughter. Because of his request, the Mihoris met with Mitsue at a hotel near Kyōto Station.

When she heard what Morikami's ideas were, Mitsue tearfully implored the Mihoris not to make her send Reiko to the United States. The young woman had received a proposal of marriage, Mitsue explained. But Mitsue realized that, in order to repay Morikami's kindness to her family, the Okamotos were obligated to provide him with care in return. She asked whether Morikami would consider the younger daughter, Akiko, in Reiko's place. After arriving back in Florida, the Mihoris explained the matter to Morikami. He refused to understand, and vented his dissatisfaction on them.

On the surface, Morikami presented an affability that complemented the smiling face that he showed upon first meeting someone. But inside, he had considerable pride and an obstinate personal style that made him inflexible. He did not conceal his displeasure when circumstances were not to his liking. Morikami, who had long lived a solitary life and who continued a hermit-like existence with farming as his only activity, had a side to him that was difficult to please.

Morikami's attempt to adopt his niece marked a low point in his relationship with the Okamotos. But after a while it seemed as if it had never happened, and the exchange of correspondence between them resumed. Sometime later, Reiko divorced her husband. Since she had previously admired America, she now hoped she could go there. But by that time, in 1968, Morikami's feelings had changed from what they had been previously. He said it was okay for Reiko to make a trip to the United States, but he did not think she should come to the US to live. He suggested that she remain with her family in Japan and wait for the opportunity to remarry.

Morikami explained to the Okamotos that while living a solitary life may make one lonely, he enjoyed a peaceful existence out in the country and close to nature. He did not feel ill at ease.

Making a Donation of His Land and Leaving Behind His Name

In the short time that George Morikami had known James Mihori, he had asked numerous times, "How do you think I can make sure my name is remembered after I am gone?" When he first heard the question, Mihori was surprised. "He was a person who would express these incredible notions. Old-timers who were born in Meiji [that is, in the late nineteenth century] are certainly different from younger people such as myself, born in Shōwa [the twentieth century]."

Finding Morikami's outlook refreshing, Mihori decided to help him make his wish a reality. "It was for a situation such as this that we happened to meet," said Mihori. They considered several ways in which Morikami might preserve his name for posterity. One idea was to donate land to a government body for use as a park or something similar for public benefit. Morikami, who did not have much ready cash compared to the considerable land that he owned, would be granted a special exemption from paying taxes on the basis of such a donation. With development in Florida surging ahead, land values in Delray Beach were on the rise. The assessment of his property was going up, along with the taxes levied on it. If he held on to his land as he had been doing, he worried that it would be confiscated for nonpayment of taxes unless he did something about it.

In the middle of the 1960s, Morikami made his first donation of property, to the State of Florida for use as an agriculture experimental station. Accordingly, from that point forward he was exempted from paying property taxes. Apart from the donation made to ease Morikami's tax burden, Morikami and Mihori decided to approach the State of Florida about a second donation, this time to vouchsafe the memory of his name. Mihori had talked with Warren Grimes, his employer, about Morikami's proposed gift. Since Grimes was an acquaintance of Florida's governor, they thought that the donation of land for a state park might be accepted.

Mihori flew to Tallahassee on the corporate jet to call on the head of the department overseeing the state park system. Upon his arrival, even before Mihori had a chance to take a seat, the department head asked, "How many acres does he [Morikami] want to donate?"

"Two hundred eighty-five acres," Mihori replied, still standing.

"The State of Florida only accepts gifts of land that are over 300 acres for the purpose of creating parks," the official explained. "Since you haven't enough land to offer, perhaps Mr. Grimes would be willing to purchase additional land with the intention of donating it, too?"

Mihori called his employer and explained the situation. "Would you buy fifteen acres to donate on George's behalf?" he asked.

Grimes refused. "Why should I be the one to buy it?" he wanted to know. "Isn't it George who wants this?"

Before Mihori ever had a chance to sit down, the meeting was over. "*Dame deshita* [It didn't work out]," Mihori said as he explained the situation to Morikami later.

"*Mō, dame deshō ka ne* [There's no way, is there?]" Morikami said despondently.

Next, Morikami approached the City of Delray Beach with the offer of land for a municipal public park. He had lived in Delray Beach for a long time and felt strongly about benefiting the city in some manner. Going to the Delray Beach city hall on Morikami's behalf, Mihori met with city commissioners to present the elderly farmer's proposed donation. Standing in its way, though, were several issues. Morikami's property was outside of the city limits; in fact, it lay at some distance from the city limits. Even if the commissioners accepted the gift, the city did not have the finances to make the necessary improvements to open the park to the public. City commissioners, too, declined to accept Morikami's offer.

"*Dame desu ka ne* [It didn't work out this time, either]," Morikami said once more, his face clouding over.

Planting Trees at the Age of Eighty

"If I Can Plant Something Today, I'll Die Happily Tomorrow"

Morikami's younger sister, Fude, passed away August 9, 1965. In the Morigami family, oldest son Sukeji (Morikami) had gone to the United States as a young man, while third son Masabei had also left home and had established his own family elsewhere in the town of Miyazu. Fourth son Yoneji had been adopted into his wife's family but had died during the Second World War. Fude, who married Motoji Ida but also inherited the Morigami family home, often wanted to consult with Morikami over family matters, and she wrote to tell him that she hoped he would return one day to live with her in the family home. He never did. Morikami probably experienced feelings of loneliness and depression, and he no doubt wept in recollecting Fude. But at age seventy-eight he did not think he could travel ever again to Japan.

Meanwhile, Morikami continued to make improvements to his property. He released fish into the pond he had made, and after obtaining black pine and maple seeds planted them around the pond's edge. As he worked, he suddenly thought about the cedar and cypress trees that he had planted in his hometown many years before. He wondered how well they had fared.

Morikami sowed loquat seeds that he had obtained from Japan. He planted peaches from Ceylon and Okinawa. He cultivated raspberries, avocados, mangos, and tangerines, and he grew peony-cherry trees and Tamba chestnuts. Black pine, soybean, and radish flourished when he sowed seeds for them, along with maple, nandina, and Uji tea. The tea plants did not survive.

"It's just eight o'clock in the morning. The weather report is for cloudy skies and showers. Today will be ideal weather for my plan to transplant the Japanese black pine and Uji tea seedlings," Morikami wrote in February 1967. He continued, "I am eighty years old and yet I plant trees. People may laugh at my foolishness. Although I may be foolish, this is my life's desire, my dream. If I can plant something today, I will have no regrets if I die tomorrow."

In the spring of that year, his cherry blossoms were gorgeous.

. . . .

On December 15, 1967, Morikami went to the federal office building in Miami, where his application for US citizenship was approved. Morikami had thought about acquiring citizenship before, but at the time there was a test on American government and history that was likely to be difficult for him, so he had hesitated. Moreover, when Morikami consulted his attorney, he was told that obtaining citizenship might cost as much as $6,000. "If it is true that it costs so much money, then someone is receiving payments under the table," he thought. "If that is the case, I don't want citizenship."

However, the truth was that Japanese who had immigrated to the US before the war had been eligible for US citizenship since 1952, according to the McCarran-Walter Act. The fee to apply was just ten dollars. Morikami learned this from Virginia Snyder, a journalist and private investigator living in the area. In 1967, Morikami's offer to donate land to the City of Delray Beach was turned down. When the proposed gift was put to a vote at a city council meeting, Virginia Snyder was there to cover the event for her newspaper. Intrigued by the generosity of the gift and appalled by the shortsightedness of the city council, Snyder sought out Morikami, after which the two became good friends.

On the day he acquired citizenship, Morikami wrote to his niece, Akiko:

This past December 15 was the greatest, most memorable day of my life. It's been a desire of mine for as long as sixty years, and now I am an American citizen, naturalized in this country. The newspaper printed a big article with a photograph and congratulated me. Friends and acquaintances were all delighted for me. . . . Even my present circumstances I owe to this country. [If I hadn't made a success in this country,] I probably couldn't have sent you money for as long as I did after the war. You and Reiko could not have finished your educations. For what I have now, both directly and indirectly . . . I owe to this country.

Feeling deep emotions, he claimed that American citizenship had been his "desire for as long as sixty years," forgetting that in 1906 his original plan had been to return to Japan after three years.

Virginia Snyder let the mayor of Delray Beach know that Morikami, having acquired US citizenship, wanted to repay the debt to America that he felt he owed by donating his property to the city and to America. As a result, Morikami was invited to a meeting of the Delray Beach City Council in early 1968. Not knowing the reason why he had been asked to attend, he sat in the first row dozing when he heard the mayor say, "It is a tremendous joy to make George Morikami honorary mayor of Delray Beach." Surprised at the unexpected mention of his name, Morikami at first was speechless. Applause from the others in attendance filled the room. While he stood to accept a certificate presented by the mayor, he smiled broadly to express his gratitude to the crowd.

A month prior to this, Hideo Kobayashi had passed away. One of the original Yamato colonists, Kobayashi came from Hyōgo Prefecture in Japan and had done landscape gardening in Ft. Lauderdale since before the war. With his death, everyone from the original group of settlers was gone. Then, on June 18, 1970, Morikami's brother Masabei also passed away. Both of his brothers and his sister who had grown to adulthood, the last of his siblings, were now gone.

Even as Morikami turned eighty-one, he continued to occupy himself with farming activities. In the spring of 1970, at the age of eighty-three, he planted thirty flowering plant seedlings and continued to cultivate avocado, mango, and papaya. The next year he bought a machine to use in weeding his pineapple field. In the previous year, the persimmon tree had borne fruit in abundance, reminding Morikami of the persimmons in his hometown and at the house in the neighborhood of Takiba where he had spent his childhood.

Now, when he grew tired and went to sleep in his house trailer, mice nibbled at his toes. Not far away, the call of an alligator could be heard.

Morikami Park and Yamato Road

When 1972 arrived, Morikami sent for a mail-order black pine that he planned to train as a *bonsai*. He also planted 5,000 red cedar saplings. "After several years, they grew into splendid six- or seven-foot-tall Christmas trees," he boasted. In his fields he planted onions and raised the small red radishes that Japanese call *hatsuka daikon* or "twenty-day" radishes. He also set out squash and *shiso* (perilla), a kind of mint. Always interested in expanding his knowledge, Morikami wrote to the Okamoto family to ask for the farming periodicals *Gendai Nōgyō* (Agriculture Today) and *Nōgyō Engei* (Agricultural Gardening) to be sent to him from Japan.

The following summer, Morikami's foot slipped as he climbed off his tractor, and he burned himself badly when his leg came into contact with the tractor's hot muffler. Despite the mishap, he did not see a doctor, but treated himself with a salve of his own concoction. "It was a miracle that I survived," he wrote the Okamotos. Because of the seriousness of the wound, for a long time he could hardly move his body and spent many days passing the time reading, the only activity he could do.

The injury eventually healed, and afterward, for the first time in a long while, Morikami took his pickup truck out for a drive. He was surprised at the volume of traffic he encountered, yet despite his apprehension, he went for a fifty-mile spin. To his mind, there were more cars on the road than ever before. Residential development also seemed to be progressing rapidly everywhere he looked. Development had come to surround Morikami's farm entirely, seeming to pressure him to give up his bucolic lifestyle. Winter visitors from other states had increased considerably in number, while college students from the Northeast crowded into Florida during their spring break from classes.

It seemed unbelievable, but when Morikami had first come to Florida in 1906, he could walk on the beach and not encounter another person, while a ship passing out at sea was an unusual sight. He wrote the Okamotos that he sometimes thought of the sea in his hometown of Miyazu; of the scenic sandbank laden with pines called Amanohashidate, the "Bridge of Heaven"; and of Chion-ji, a temple in the nearby neighborhood of Monju.

> When it gets to be summer, I think of Monju. I used to shove off [from there] to fish in the Aso Lagoon [a part of Miyazu Bay] for horse mackerel, flathead, goby, octopus and other fish. In front of Chion-ji temple was a hotel with a restaurant. Local specialty products such as "wisdom" *mochi* [*mochi* with sweet bean paste inside] and *dengaku* [grilled *tofu* with a *miso* glaze] were sold there. Since I liked them both, I splurged my five *sen*. At the time there weren't many visitors in summer and the place was deserted. As there was no bridge to it, we took a boat to the Bridge of Heaven.

Both the Bridge of Heaven as Morikami remembered it from his youth and Yamato before its demise were quiet, peaceful places. Had he returned to his hometown, Morikami probably would have looked around in astonishment at the changes that had undoubtedly taken place there. He witnessed overwhelming change all around him in Florida, too, yet he managed to hang on to his own way of life.

Morikami dreaded the loss of solitude and wanted to go away and leave development in Florida behind. Once he longed to go to Brazil, where he dreamed of opening up new farmland, but gave up the plan. Little by little his strength was diminishing; his physical condition was poor, and he often had to stop what he was doing to rest. There were even times when he could not stand. In order to plant his pineapples, Morikami got down on his hands and knees and was somehow able dig furrows in the dirt while dragging himself around. Nevertheless, he energetically defended his fields from the rabbits and field mice that sometimes invaded them. Once, when his plant beds were raided by a flock of blackbirds, Morikami was able to shoot as many as thirty of them.

Morikami, who had made the decision to donate almost all of the land that he cultivated, wrote about the property in a letter addressed to his niece Reiko. He told her that shortly after the end of the war he had been making a living working as a tenant farmer.

Happily, as I had a little bit of profit from farming, I managed to scrape together some money to buy land. I was able to buy the land on credit. I bought and sold land, and one time owned nearly 1,000 acres. But then I had a hard time paying the property taxes. Because land became more and more expensive, . . . I quit and only sold a little. Currently, what money I have has come from land sales, not from farming. I've donated some land to the state, and given away some to friends. Left over, I have 150 acres. Thanks to the current land boom, I am not starving, but living comfortably.

In his letter, Morikami mentioned donating land, but at the time, his donation of property to be used as a park had not yet taken place. If any future donations were to become a park, Morikami believed, his name could endure as that of the park. His name would not carry on, however, if he were unable to make such a donation.

So far Morikami's offer to donate parkland had been turned down by both the state and the city, leaving Palm Beach County as the only possible recipient that remained. Accordingly, James Mihori once again conferred with Warren Grimes, his employer, on the best way for the donation to become a reality.

Grimes introduced Mihori to a county commissioner who was also a card-playing buddy of his. Through this commissioner, Mihori was granted an opportunity to explain Morikami's proposal before the full board. Since Palm Beach County operated over twenty parks at the time, a specific justification for creating another one was necessary. Accordingly, Mihori told the commissioners, "The state of Florida has many counties, but if the county commissioners accept Morikami's gift, and Morikami Park becomes a reality, then Palm Beach County will have something that the others do not, the only park with a Japanese name." It was an ingenious argument that persuaded the commissioners to accept Morikami's gift.

The property, donated in several separate gifts, ultimately was consolidated with the adjacent parcel that he had previously donated to the state for an agricultural extension station. Together, they formed Morikami Park—in all, 180 acres.

Since Morikami's land, which he had purchased over a period of years, was in several parcels, a careful survey of the property had to be carried out by the county after the donation was finalized. Certain out-parcels had to be consolidated in order to create, to the extent possible, one contiguous land area. For another thing, a road merely to provide access to the park had to be constructed. Even in this matter Mihori negotiated with county commissioners, successfully preparing for the construction of a road that would eventually continue into the next county. Mihori's activism also helped prepare for the construction of a road from the expressway to the park.

In the 1960s construction of Interstate 95 along the Atlantic seaboard was making progress in Florida, and in the 1970s the interstate opened to traffic in the Delray Beach area. This made a road connecting Mori-kami Park with the highway a possibility.

A public hearing was held to determine a name for the road. At the hearing, local residents and officials voiced their opinions, and offi-cials of the county parks and recreation department proposed Yamato Road as a fitting name. These parties explained that the former site of a settlement of Japanese called the Yamato Colony was located nearby. Their suggestion was approved, and the new Yamato Road, identified prominently on signage above highway exit ramps, went west from the expressway in the direction of Morikami Park, about five miles away.

Settling the matter of the donation of his property probably gave Morikami peace of mind. Morikami told the Okamoto family in Japan, "[This] has been my long-cherished desire, to express my gratitude for all of the advantages I have received [in the United States]." On the other hand, he wrote, "I made a similar proposal to my hometown of Miyazu and received no reply."

"I'm a Millionaire"

On March 15, 1974, a ceremony to dedicate Morikami Park took place at the park site. Palm Beach County parks department officials gath-ered at a spot with nothing but sandy soil underfoot. Even Morikami, who ordinarily disliked appearing in public or in the press, was present, dressed in a rarely worn suit and tie for his major role as the guest of honor.

A Palm Beach County commissioner expressed his gratitude for the land that Morikami had donated to the county, then exchanged a cordial handshake with the elderly farmer whose joints were swollen after long years of working his fields. As he took a shovel in hand during a light drizzle, Morikami's beaming face was captured by the photographer of a local newspaper at the moment of the groundbreaking that began the dedication ceremony.

Morikami, who was featured in several newspaper reports, became quite famous as a result of his gift of land to the county. He received close to 100 letters from other parts of the US as well as Japan, but while he read them all, he was far from happy to receive them. Instead, he was appalled. "Actually, even ten of those letters would not have made me happy," he wrote. "Nearly all were asking for money." Morikami grew to fear being kidnapped because of the reports of his wealth, and from that time forward, he asked newspapers not to write about him and refused permission for them to do so.

When construction work began on the land he donated, Morikami wrote to the Okamotos that in front of the public he pretended to be uninterested in what was happening on the property "because [he had] already given it away." Often, though, when no one was around he drove his tractor over to the site in the park where a museum building was under construction. Morikami wanted to keep track of its progress. Moreover, he even had a copy of the plans for the park attached to the wall of his house trailer.

On February 25, 1974, Shohbi Kamikama, another of the former Yamato colonists, passed away at the age of eighty-three. Kamikama had come to Florida from New York in 1917. Like Morikami, he also had lived a simple lifestyle for many years. Situated amid rows of towering condominiums, Kamikama's dilapidated residence built of cement blocks was crammed with piles of old newspapers but had hardly any furniture. Toward the end of his life, he lived alone, reading those old Japanese newspapers that seemed to be stacked as high as the ceiling, while an elderly Bahamian woman who lived in a small house next door took care of him as his common-law wife.

A newspaper reporter who visited Kamikama wrote that when he saw how the eighty-two-year-old lived, he could not help but feel sorry him. Although Kamikama, like Morikami, lived a lifestyle that appeared at first glance to be mired in poverty, in truth he was a wealthy landowner. As he grew his vegetable crops, Kamikama also bought land a little at a time along Highway US 1 for as little as thirty dollars an acre. When he sold the land to a large supermarket in Boca Raton, he pocketed a substantial sum.

Living frugally, Kamikama limited his extravagances to items such as foodstuffs ordered from Japan and Japanese-language newspapers mailed to him from California. A mostly unfriendly individual, Kamikama was the last of the Yamato colonists to live within the geographic area that was known as Yamato. However, Morikami had almost no contact with him.

During his lifetime, Kamikama sold land he owned for less than its market value, and his personal wealth seemed to diminish, yet at the time of his death he owned thirteen acres and had a bank account. According to a 1935 will found in a bank safety deposit box, he had two sisters living in his hometown in Kagoshima Prefecture, in southwestern Japan. These family members were able to realize little from his estate in comparison to what lawyers divided among themselves. On top of that, the niece and nephew of Kamikama's common-law wife also sued the estate for some of the inheritance.

The elder sister in Kagoshima who received Kamikama's ashes unexpectedly when he died was hardly close to her brother and did not know very much about him. Relatives knew little other than that he had gone to the US to receive an education and had died there. Morikami was upset with the way that Kamikama's assets were managed by his attorneys. Following Kamikama's death, of all the former Yamato colonists, only Morikami remained.

The Hands of an Old Man Planting Pineapples

Late in life, Morikami sometimes puffed out his chest and boasted, "I'm a millionaire!" He was indeed a man of means who had accumulated wealth and owned extensive acreage. But his lifestyle was far from that of a millionaire. He did not at all possess the flair that had come to characterize southern Florida, with its succession of showy resorts on the beach.

George Morikami lived in a dilapidated trailer that he had placed on his land after trees had been cleared and at about the same time that an uneven gravel road was put in. Nearly every day he drove his old Ford tractor from the trailer to his fields, and as he did so, around him time seemed to stop.

In March 1975, a Japanese man came to visit and see for himself how Morikami lived his life. He was Akira Suwa, a photographer for the *Palm Beach Post*, a local newspaper. One day Suwa's editor said to him, "In Delray Beach is a Japanese who owns a large tract of land. Until now we have tried repeatedly to photograph him, but he has turned down every request. Even our best photographer couldn't get a picture. You are Japanese, why don't you go interview him?"

After graduating from Tōkyō University of Agriculture, Suwa had traveled to the US and found work in Japanese garden design and maintenance in Tampa, Florida. Just before this, in 1962, yachtsman Ken'ichi Horie had completed his solo voyage across the Pacific Ocean. News of his success was the talk of Japan. Young Suwa, influenced by Horie's feat, left Japan for foreign shores hoping that he, too, could have an adventure of some kind.

The company for which he worked, however, went bankrupt and closed after a couple of years, bringing Suwa to a point in his life when he had to think hard about his future. He looked into photography, an interest he had always had, and sought employment at a photography store in Plant City, east of Tampa. That move opened opportunities for Suwa. He became a news photographer working first for papers in Tampa and St. Petersburg. In 1974 he relocated to Palm Beach on Florida's Atlantic coast to work for the *Palm Beach Post*. Until his editor mentioned the Yamato Colony and George Morikami, Suwa had known nothing about them.

Because of work assignments during regular working hours, Suwa first tried visiting Morikami on his day off. But just at the time when he hoped to see the elderly farmer, Morikami suffered a decline in health from arthritis and stomach ulcers. For two or three days he could not see anyone.

Since he was aware that Morikami behaved cautiously toward those he did not know, Suwa decided not to carry his camera so as not to give himself away as a newspaper man until he identified himself as one.

Introducing himself to Morikami, he said, "I am Suwa, a photographer for the Palm Beach newspaper who is from Japan."

Morikami, against all expectations, smiled broadly and greeted Suwa cheerfully. Their first meeting was unusual only in that Morikami always responded in English when Suwa spoke to him in Japanese. While speaking in English about recent events, Morikami, who had a special interest in agricultural techniques, was delighted to learn that Suwa was a graduate of Tōkyō University of Agriculture.

During their conversation, Suwa came to realize that Morikami understood Japanese perfectly well. He soon came to know why: on the table in Morikami's house trailer lay a copy of a popular Japanese-English, English-Japanese dictionary. In addition, books and magazines were crammed together on a bookshelf that was overflowing.

Visible on the spines of some of the volumes were the titles of Japanese-language novels like *Arasuka Monogatari* by Jirō Nitta, (An Alaskan Tale; about early twentieth-century Japanese mining pioneer Frank Yasuda), *Yoshitsune* by Ryōtarō Shiba (about a twelfth-century *samurai* who remains one of Japan's most popular historical figures), and *Kōkotsu no Hito* by Sawako Ariyoshi (The Twilight Years; about issues of aging in contemporary Japanese society). Nonfiction titles included those of agriculture-related books such as *Mame Bonsai Nyūmon* (Introduction to Miniature Dwarfed Potted Trees) and *Gendai Nōsei Mondō* (Agricultural Management Q and A), plus books on Tenrikyō, the Okamoto family's religious faith. Suwa could also see special issues of the periodical *Kingu*.

Among the English-language books were many related to agricultural practice, like *The New Garden Encyclopedia* and *Organic Plant Protection*. Others, such as *Sane Living in a Mad World: A Guide to the Organic Way of Life*, brought to mind Morikami's lifestyle.

Regarding Morikami's character, Suwa formed the impression that he "was an extremely decent individual, someone who was kindhearted," but inwardly Suwa was appalled that in appearance, Morikami "had the look of a beggar, without question." Dressed in a dirty shirt and short pants, he had thin, wispy hair and a scraggly beard. For that matter, his narrow four-room house trailer was untidy as well.

After their initial encounter, Suwa often dropped by Morikami's place without his camera on days off, engaging the elderly farmer in

George Morikami in his house trailer, 1975 (photo by Akira Suwa).

conversation about pineapple cultivation and similar topics. Morikami had an electric fan in his house trailer but no air conditioner, and he always left his door open. He had a regular bed but did not use it, always choosing instead to nap on a smaller bed. To Morikami, who was short in stature, it was all he needed.

Scattered about in confusion on top of a cluttered table in his trailer were containers of condiments, a jar of Nescafé instant coffee, an aluminum plate, and other odds and ends. At the door of the trailer, what appeared to be *bonsai*-like pines grew in pots and buckets. Morikami seemed to live as if he were off by himself deep in a forest, yet he did have contact with people who visited him to buy pineapples and bananas that he harvested from his fields.

Observing Morikami's disorderly home and way of life, Suwa felt sorry for him. Morikami needed someone to look after him—that much was clear. While Suwa couldn't assume that responsibility, at least he could do some cleaning. He supposed he could recruit his wife to help and go to Morikami's trailer to straighten it up. When Suwa discussed the idea with Morikami, the elderly farmer said that he did not mind if Suwa's wife and four-year-old daughter also came to clean for him. Morikami was cordial toward Mrs. Suwa. To the daughter he exclaimed several times, "What a cute little boy."

Morikami at age eighty-eight alone in his field planting pineapples (photo by Akira Suwa).

After nearly four months of such visits, Suwa broached the subject of capturing images of Morikami with his camera. "Coming here from Japan, leaving behind this land as a legacy—what you've accomplished is truly remarkable. Shouldn't I be taking photographs of you?" he asked. "Okay," Morikami replied, willingly giving Suwa his consent.

On the first day of photography, Suwa stuck with Morikami in whatever he did, snapping his shutter continuously throughout the day beginning around 4:00 a.m. After getting out of bed in the morning and eating his breakfast, Morikami loaded a wooden crate filled with the stiff-leafed crowns of pineapple fruit onto the cargo bed of his Ford tractor and drove out to the field to plant them. As Suwa rode behind him on the tractor, one of the wheels struck something in the road, and the photographer fell off the tractor backward. Suwa had the wind knocked out of him and for a moment couldn't catch his breath, but Morikami, who was facing straight ahead, did not notice and continued driving.

Suwa slowly picked himself up off the ground and chased after the tractor, managing somehow to jump back on. When they arrived at their destination, Morikami took the wood crate from the tractor and, doubled over, carried it to the middle of the field that spread out in all directions like a soccer court in the wilderness. The blood vessels stood out on his arms as he carried the wood crate; his arms seemed muscular in comparison to the rest of his body, gaunt as it was. His hands, planting the pineapple crowns with their spiny green leaves, were etched with the lines of age. His joints were swollen, as were his fingertips, so much so that the flesh partially buried the edges of his fingernails.

Morikami worked at his own pace planting the pineapple crowns in the sandy soil. When it suited him, he moved about wearing only his socks on his feet rather than the boots that he also had with him. He had not packed a lunch, but around noon he instead produced a bottle of an inexpensive wine, MD 20/20, to drink from. Afterward, he lay down on the ground in his clothes and took a nap. A small dog that he owned came sniffing around his face.

After an hour or so, he woke up and once again returned to the field. He worked until dusk began to settle, then returned home on his tractor. When he wasn't working in the field, Morikami sometimes sat in the living room of his house trailer and read a book.

During the period when Suwa was photographing him, Morikami celebrated his eighty-ninth birthday. A Palm Beach County commissioner visited him with a birthday cake to congratulate him. Morikami, who greeted the commissioner on the occasion dressed in brown slacks

Planting pineapples, 1975 (photo by Akira Suwa).

and an orange shirt, catnapped whenever a moment presented itself, even while in conversation with his guest. He spoke exuberantly about Japanese food, telling his visitor, "I like fish, no matter what kind it is."

Even when Suwa had other assignments, he sometimes stopped by Morikami's trailer for no particular reason if he was close enough. In this way eight months elapsed from Suwa's first meeting with Morikami to the end of the photo-taking sessions.

The End of a Long Dream

In May 1975, Morikami's tractor overturned in a ditch while he was driving. Luckily, he was able to crawl out from under it; unluckily, no one else was nearby to provide assistance to him. Mostly crawling, he gradually made his way to the nearest house, half a mile away.

In July, two months later, Morikami looked back at his exchange of correspondence with the Okamotos in a letter to his niece Reiko. "I have been writing to all of you for nearly thirty years. We have exchanged hundreds of letters, and it would be a shame to destroy them, so I don't know what to do," Morikami wrote. "If it's okay, I will send all that I have to you. Someday they will provide you with certain information, and will be good material for reminiscing about the way things used to be." Morikami had kept all of the letters that were from the Okamotos, who in turn had kept all of the letters that Morikami had sent to them for close to three decades.

On February 28, 1976, Virginia Snyder's husband, Ross, paid a visit to Morikami, whose previously strong body had grown frail. The Snyders were good friends with Morikami, and on this day Ross Snyder had gone to check up on him to see how he was doing. He found that Morikami was so weak that he could not get out of bed.

Snyder helped Morikami to sit up and take a few sips of the chicken soup he had brought. Morikami asked Snyder to read him a letter he had received. The letter was from the Internal Revenue Service, Snyder told Morikami, "asking if he [Morikami] wanted to pay a portion of his income tax ahead of time. Morikami said that he did not want to pay the money early. Once previously, he had paid too much ahead of time and had nothing but trouble getting the money back. Because of that experience he was adamant that he was not going to make the same mistake again.

After Snyder left, Art Pickering, Morkami's neighbor and acquaintance of many years, also stopped by to see how he was fairing. Pickering understood well that even though the state of Morikami's health was not good, he did not want to see a doctor. In the evening, Morikami asked Pickering to make him a tomato sandwich with plenty of mayonnaise. Pickering did, and he ate it all. Pickering then stayed at his neighbor's side until two o'clock the next morning, February 29, when he returned home. Five hours later he went back to Morikami's residence. In the interim, he discovered, Morikami had passed away.

In a letter to his niece Akiko Okamoto written shortly before his death, Morikami calculated his age in the Japanese manner. "I am 90 years old," he wrote. "Seventy years have elapsed [since I came to this country]. I worked hard, but have nothing to show for it. It was all just a long dream I had."

When Suwa heard about Morikami's death after returning from a tennis tournament he had been covering for the paper, he showed the photographs he had taken up to that point to his editor—Morikami planting pineapples in the sandy field, Morikami's dog nosing around him as he lay on the ground napping, Morikami in front of the small electric fan in his house trailer, and others. Suwa's black-and-white images capturing the farmer's many sides would soon appear in the pages of his newspaper.

Morikami, who had donated all but fifteen acres of the land he owned, left behind an estate consisting of a few personal possessions. Generally speaking, these possessions made it difficult to believe that he had been a rich man. An inventory of Morikami's assets included: the 1974 house trailer that he used as his residence; the 1955 Pontiac trailer that he had previously occupied; a 1963 Ford pickup truck that somehow still ran, if not very well; and a 1969 Volkswagen minibus that did not run at all. Among Morikami's farming equipment were the Ford tractor that he thought of as his "right-hand," unused tires from another smaller Ford tractor, tractor attachments such as a harrow and a plow, and buckets for hauling dirt. In addition, he owned a lawn mower, an electric saw, a sprayer, and a variety of other small farm implements.

Roji-en, the Morikami Museum's Japanese garden (photo by Ryusuke Kawai).

Nonfarming possessions included a 1975 Panasonic color television, which in those days, cost around $390, a copy machine, and a small typewriter.

All the land that Morikami had donated during his lifetime for the purpose of a park was nearly 200 acres in total. As the park was gradually developed, construction moved forward. A second pond on the property came to be a central feature. On an island that seemed to float in the center of the pond, a Japanese house was built in imitation of Katsura Imperial Villa in Kyōto. This house was to become the museum, and exhibits on modern Japanese lifestyle and customs and a corner for photographs telling the history of the Yamato Colony and the circumstances of its founding were in the planning stages.

As a result, one year and four months after Morikami's death, on June 25, 1977, Morikami Park opened to the public. In September of the same year, Delray Beach, the city in which Morikami had lived for many years, and his hometown of Miyazu established a sister-city relationship. Several years afterward, county officials unveiled a proposal to develop the park further, and in 1993 a new museum building with a Japanese-style roof opened, as well as a new park entrance. The new museum features a theater and galleries for the display of Japanese art and antiques. An elegant tea hut for the practice of tea ceremony, which was open to a viewing gallery to allow an audience to observe the preparation of tea, was built entirely within the museum building. In funding the museum building, a large sum of money was collected as a donation from Miyazu. Other funding sources included the State of Florida, Palm Beach County, and numerous corporations and private individuals both in the United States and Japan.

In 2001, Hoichi Kurisu, a landscape designer with experience designing Japanese gardens, adopted features of different gardens in Japan to create a garden at Morikami Park that linked them together as a uniform whole. A stone monument made in America of Georgia granite and designed after a stone lantern called the Wisdom Ring (Chie no Wa), near one end of Amanohashidate in Miyazu, was also placed in the garden. Ornamental carp swim in the pond; *bonsai* are on display; and, in January and February, cherry blossoms are in bloom.

The garden seems to cool the hot, humid air that dampens this region, and people burdened by spiritual and emotional problems visit looking for peace of mind. A quiet, healing space, the garden envelops those who walk in it.

Visitors can sample Japanese cuisine in the highly popular café, and from the open terrace they can enjoy a panoramic view of the garden surrounding the lake. Throughout the year, various seasonal events occur, including *taiko* drum performances and *ikebana* demonstrations, while lectures on Japanese culture are also given.

In the garden, weddings and other similar events occur. Kim Kobayashi, the grandson of Hideo Kobayashi, one of the original Yamato colonists who moved to Ft. Lauderdale during the war, held his wedding in Morikami Park.

On November 20, 2005, a celebration commemorating 100 years since the establishment of the Yamato Colony was held at the park. There, the descendants of former members of the colony and their families, numbering over fifty participants, gathered for Yamato Centennial Day. Descendants of Henry Kamiya came from California and

Florida, while Sumiko Kobayashi, eldest daughter of Oscar Kobayashi, also attended.

The descendants of Mitsusaburo Oki, from Japan, and Kazuaki Ida, son of Morikami's younger sister Fude Ida, from Morikami's hometown of Miyazu, traveled the farthest to attend. Looking at photographs that were taken of the former colony, some of the attendees of Yamato Centennial Day felt a sense of nostalgia, while others felt astonishment and wonder as they contemplated their roots in a small Florida community.

What has been referred to as Morikami Park is formally called the Morikami Museum and Japanese Gardens. Palm Beach County and a not-for-profit corporation, Morikami Inc., share responsibilities for operating the park.

Separated from the garden is an area of the park for active recreational pursuits centered around the Lake Biwa Pavilion. A lake is situated here with picnicking facilities beside it. Morikami previously lived in his house trailer on this site, and the lake was originally created in imitation of Lake Biwa in Japan.

Although Morikami was not able to realize his plan to create a park with an orchard, which he had worked hard to accomplish, his farm nevertheless was repurposed in such a stunning manner that he could never have imagined it. "I wish I could have shown Morikami-san this," said James Mihori with emotion. Both Mihoris were involved with Morikami Park's governance since before it opened to the public and for several decades afterward.

Morikami may have made plans ahead of time regarding burial arrangements after his death. In 1970, some six years before he passed away, his younger brother Masabei Morigami had a tomb built at Chigenji, the Morigami family temple in Miyazu. Morigami asked his elder brother whether the family should inter his remains in this family tomb. "'How can we have your name engraved among those of generations of our ancestors?' [Masabei] asked me," Morikami wrote in a letter to the Okamotos. "I am an old person who is as independent as a floating weed. I have made my own plans regarding a gravesite."

But Morikami seems not to have let anyone know what his wishes were. In the end, some of Morikami's cremated remains were interred at Morikami Park. The Okamotos in Kyōto also took charge of a portion of them. They erected a gravestone for Morikami at a cemetery in Shiga Prefecture near Lake Biwa in Japan and interred the cremains they received there.

Despite the Okamotos' arrangements, the Ida family, which had inherited the Morigami family home, had Morikami's name engraved on the Morigami family tomb at Chigenji. In the same tomb, Morikami's parents also repose. What is more, the Sakai family tomb where Jo Sakai's ancestors are interred is also located in this cemetery.

In Florida's Morikami Park, ashes repose beneath a gravestone dedicated to Sukeji Morikami that occupies a corner of the garden. Next to it stands a grave marker engraved with the names of both Jo Sakai and Mitsusaburo Oki. The ashes of Jo Sakai, who planned the Yamato Colony but succumbed to illness while his goals for it were only partially achieved, are buried in a West Palm Beach cemetery located twenty miles north of the park.

Palm Beach was where Henry Flagler, the wealthy industrialist who brought Sakai and the other colonists to settle in southern Florida, and who promoted a plan to extend his railroad all the way to Key West, built a magnificent chalk-white mansion and lived there to the end of his life. This fifty-five-room building that he named Whitehall later became the Flagler Museum and now is a proud emblem of the Gilded Age of America and the development of Florida.

Around the time that both Flagler's railroad plan and the Yamato Colony began, Florida's population was 528,000, but by the time of Morikami's death, it had ballooned to 8.6 million. Developers built condominiums and hotels in a row along the beach, while land surrounding these structures and even inland came to be developed as resorts and residential communities. Seen from the air, new communities spread like the heavily laden branches of fruit trees, branching out among the swampland and canals.

Today, traces of the Yamato Colony are nowhere in evidence. Even nearby Yamato Rock, which the Japanese from the former colony sometimes visited for picnic outings, is visible only as an indistinct, low-lying form on the beach. George Morikami, who came to work in southern Florida without understanding that Yamato was a result of Henry Flagler's grand plan in which he himself played a role, used to visit this rocky outcropping with the other colonists when he was a young man. From that time he never returned to Japan, but lived out his life for more than seventy years in his own unique manner, leaving behind the name of Morikami etched indelibly on the land. And, as a consequence, the name of Yamato has also remained in Florida as well.

Epilogue

Ukyō Ward, Kyōto

George Morikami, who hardly went anywhere other than Miyazu and Florida, spent some time in the city of Kyōto before leaving Japan. Morikami would take walks in the neighborhood of Kyōgoku, the last place in Japan of which he would have memories. A couple of miles to the west of Kyōgoku is a station called Saiin on a private railway line.

In September 2012, I visited Saiin looking for the residence of Hatsu Onizawa, about whom Morikami had written to the Okamotos more than fifty years earlier. I wondered whether her family continued to live here after half a century and worried that they did not. I walked back and forth on different streets, looking for the address. Then, at last, among the houses on a narrow side street, I discovered a nameplate reading, "Odani," Hatsu's surname following her marriage. I pushed the button on the intercom and soon was stating my business.

Granting me an interview was Hatsu's grandson Hideyo Odani, a quiet gentleman of approximately seventy years of age. Apologizing for my rudeness in visiting unexpectedly, I explained my purpose for being there. He agreed to speak to me, answering a few questions that day and again nine months later when I called on him after finding out more about Morikami's circumstances.

When George Morikami was near the age of seventy, he wrote to Hatsu Odani. Whenever he looked back over his life, Morikami could not ignore memories of his first love. When I considered how often he had written to relatives and friends, it struck me that he must have written to Hatsu as well. But in his correspondence with the Okamotos, Morikami never mentioned receiving even one reply from Hatsu to any letters he may have written to her. Could it be that Hatsu thought she was receiving expressions of affection from someone who was behaving like a stalker and, finding them troubling, never reciprocated?

With such concerns in mind, I tried questioning Odani closely regarding correspondence from Morikami, whether or not there was any and what its contents might have been. Odani answered, "I know that letters came from Morikami-san." He also said, "Grandmother was moved by what seemed to be feelings of nostalgia as she read them."

Surely, then, all the correspondence could not have been one-way. Is it possible that the two of them made a promise of some kind before Morikami went to the US? Although there was no way of knowing for certain what their relationship was like, it seemed apparent that Hatsu remembered their time together with fondness.

Morikami's life had not been simple, and neither had Hatsu's, although, of course, her path was different from his. In 1909, three years after Morikami had gone to the United States, Hatsu graduated from the girls' high school in Miyazu and married with her parents' blessing. Hatsu's spouse was Naotada Odani, who was also from Miyazu and who worked for Japan National Railways; his family had been *samurai* retainers of the Miyazu Domain for generations. Despite this background, however, they were less well-off than the Onizawas, Hatsu's own family, who were master carpenters and relatively affluent.

When the couple married, Hatsu moved to Kōbe to live close to her husband's work. From there, they moved to Yonago, Tottori Prefecture, where they lived for a time before returning to Kōbe. Odani then retired from the railroad and took a job with the City of Kōbe's transportation bureau. Afterward he went into private business, opening a printing company that Hatsu helped to operate. Finally, they ran a toy store together.

In 1938, Hatsu's husband died of illness at the age of fifty-two. Prior to this the couple's eldest daughter, Fumiko, had married and left home, followed by their second daughter, Hanae. The youngest child, a son named Naotaka, had entered Tōkyō University School of Agriculture.

Because Hatsu was left alone in Kōbe after the death of her husband, she went to live with Naotaka in Tōkyō.

Shortly afterward, however, Naotaka also contracted an illness and passed away in his third year at Tōkyō University. Hatsu, who had less of a reason to remain in Tōkyō than she had in Kōbe, went to live with the family of her second daughter, Hanae, in Shanghai, China. When Hanae's husband, Kuniyo, was drafted, the family moved to Port Arthur, where he was assigned. Feeling uneasy about the situation in China and the eventual result of the war, Hatsu decided to return by herself to Japan and to her hometown of Miyazu.

Hatsu lived by herself in a tenement in Miyazu while the situation in China deteriorated. Hatsu's daughter Hanae, accompanied by Hatsu's two grandchildren, soon came seeking shelter with her. When the war ended, Kuniyo was repatriated to Miyazu as well. Because rations were often scarce, he rented a house and farm fields on the outskirts of town where Hatsu continued to live with the family.

In 1950, Kuniyo's family moved to Yokohama. Hatsu was alone again, but only for a brief period. Hanae took ill and returned to Miyazu, where she and her children lived with Hatsu once more. Hanae soon passed away, however. Kuniyo married a second time, but because he had previously been adopted into the Odani family as heir to the Odani name, he continued to welcome Hatsu as part of his household.

With Hatsu also making the move, the Odani family relocated to the city of Kyōto in 1960. After Kuniyo's death, his eldest son assumed headship of the Odani family. Hatsu would share her declining years with the family of her biological grandson Hideyo Odani.

Morikami's correspondence with Hatsu seems to have begun just before the family's move to Kyōto. In June 1982, more than twenty years after she had received the first of his letters, Hatsu passed away just prior to her ninety-first birthday. It had been six years since Morikami's own death.

"Actually, I too sent a letter to Morikami-san," Odani told me. "It was when I was in my third year of middle school or first year of high school, I don't remember exactly. At the time I much admired America. Morikami-san sent my grandmother an article about himself from an American newspaper. I saw it, too. To think that I actually knew someone who had achieved that kind of success. I wrote to him that I wanted to go to America, too. But from Morikami-san came a reply saying, 'It's not worth coming all the way from Japan to do this kind of hard work.'"

Odani smiled. Reflected in his eyes was his conviction that Morikami, who had been mentioned in an American newspaper, had been a great man. When Hatsu replied to Morikami about the newspaper article, her grandson enclosed his own letter in the envelope.

"I still have some correspondence from Morikami-san to my grandmother," Odani said, showing me three pieces of mail. Their cancelation stamps were from December 1960, December 1965, and December 1966. All were New Year's greeting cards, the words on them almost the same in every instance. The 1961 New Year's greeting was in an attractive card bearing the image of a palm tree with the ocean behind it. It was inside an envelope with "Hatsuko Odani-sama" written on the front. Printed horizontally on the card appeared the phrase "Season's Greetings," while written vertically by hand was, "Best Wishes in the New Year. Praying for your good health, Sukeji Morikami." It was beautifully written in pen in a single line of text with "George S. Morikami, P.O. Box 1375, Delray Beach, Florida" rubber-stamped next to it.

On the New Year's card for 1966, Morikami had written "age eighty years" next to his name. Perhaps he had sent New Year's greetings every year as a matter of course. It seemed to me that, other than the New Year's cards, he must have also sent more personalized letters to which Hatsu would have replied. I was told that, like Morikami, Hatsu enjoyed reading and possessed beautiful penmanship.

While speaking with Odani-san, I tried to imagine what would be in any letters that the two of them might have exchanged. Could such letters have included reminiscences of their hometown and the time they once shared with one another?

POSTSCRIPT

In 1961, the Japanese-language book *Beikoku Nikkeijin Hyakunen Shi: Zaibei Nikkeijin Hatten Jinshiroku* (One Hundred Years of Japanese American History: Individuals Who Contributed to the Growth of the Japanese American Community) was published to commemorate the one-hundredth anniversary of the signing of the US-Japan Treaty of Amity and Commerce. Shin Nichibei Shimbunsha, a Los Angeles publishing company that at the time produced a Japanese-language newspaper, compiled and issued the book.

At 1,431 pages, the size of a large dictionary, *Beikoku Nikkeijin Hyakunen Shi* is a unique work that traces in detail the movement of first-generation Japanese immigrants throughout the United States. Rather than providing generalities, it is specific in identifying Japanese who were the first to settle an area—Idaho, for example. As much as possible, each section of the book provides individuals' names and such details about them as where they were from (with names of prefectures, hometowns, etc.) as well as dates of birth and other relevant facts.

Japanese began immigrating abroad at a time when undeveloped regions still existed everywhere in the United States, a time when much of the country remained a blank map. Reading through the book, one understands how Japanese came to this country in large numbers after the Meiji Restoration, how they spread out to various places as if filling in the blank map, and how they came to stay in those places.

Emigrating from Japan to America and leaving behind all that was familiar and safe for an uncertain future was a risky endeavor that required a strong will. Few Japanese immigrants understood English, and they had no assurances of success. Yet they accepted the challenge of establishing new lives for themselves in a new world. At the same time, unexpected forces beyond their control arose to affect the circumstances of their lives; Japan and America underwent drastic change in the first half of the twentieth century. For Americans of Japanese ancestry, hardly a worse state of affairs could have arisen than the war between Japan and the United States.

On the other hand, the early twentieth century was also a time when the first-generation immigrant who was willing to make the effort had the potential to reap huge rewards in America. Many of them did so, becoming successful individuals who rode the wave of opportunity with skill. In the pages of *Beikoku Nikkeijin Hyakunen Shi*, the lives of many first-generation immigrants and second-generation Japanese Americans tell of such dynamism.

If we seek traces of Japanese immigrants in Florida, many of the Yamato colonists, including Jo Sakai, remembered feelings of being "stuck" in Japan, where few opportunities were available to them. After pursuing an education in the US, Sakai acted on his aspirations and established the colony in southern Florida. At the time, the United States had surpassed the countries of Europe economically and, of course, was continuing to grow and develop. Henry Morrison Flagler, the wealthy industrialist who ran Standard Oil Company together with John D. Rockefeller, set out to develop the Florida peninsula and built a railroad all the way to Key West. As the colony endeavor founded by Jo Sakai and others got under way, it was funded by profits from Tango *chirimen*, the silk crepe industry of the Tango Peninsula that had parallels to Flagler's great undertaking.

The colony, which was founded on lofty principles and with noble goals in mind, thrived initially with its successful crops. But before long, many of the colonists, due to the harshness of the natural environment and their own sudden wealth from the rise in land prices, gave up their farms and left Yamato.

One Japanese farmer, George Sukeji Morikami, immigrated to the US in order to escape the pain of rejection in love as well as to improve his position financially. These reasons were unconnected to any altruistic purpose for establishing a colony. Deep inside, Morikami vowed to achieve success while abroad, return to Japan, plant an orchard, and again propose marriage to the young woman to whom he had lost his heart. For various reasons, though, he was unable to realize these plans as he hoped, and he never once returned to Japan. Instead, by the time of his death in 1976 he was the last of the Yamato colonists still remaining in Florida's Palm Beach County, where the colony had been located.

There, Morikami was able to have his name immortalized as that of a park located on land that he had purchased a little at a time and donated to the local community. Related to this achievement, Delray Beach, where the park is located, and Morikami's hometown of Miyazu are sister cities that today share an exchange program for high school students.

In this way, Morikami became an exemplary individual who brought together the countries of Japan and the United States through the sister cities of Delray Beach and Miyazu and through Morikami Park and Museum, all of which create opportunities to introduce Japanese culture to Florida. By comparison, though, details connected with Morikami—what he really thought, how he lived his life, etc.—remain largely unknown. For example, he contributed funds toward the rebuilding of an elementary school in Miyazu, yet no record of his contribution remains there. Thinking this strange, I searched for such documentation in different places, finding it at last in the library of Florida Atlantic University.

An appropriate point of departure in any examination of the link between Florida and Miyazu would be the life and ideas of Jo Sakai, who was also from Morikami's hometown. Yet records or other resources pertaining to Sakai do not exist in Miyazu in any form whatsoever. Nor is there evidence of any interest in the colony founder and entrepreneur either in his hometown or anywhere else. Even though he graduated from New York University, Sakai was unknown there. On the strength of research materials at the Morikami Museum, I visited the library at New York University. There, I did discover the name "Joe Sakai" on an old, incomplete graduation list. This at least confirmed that he had once been a student there.

The grandson of another of the early colonists, Hideo Kobayashi, made a remark to me that sent me off in another direction for information. The grandson, Kim Kobayashi, said, "I don't know anything about my roots." Armed with the address that appeared on Hideo Kobayashi's passport when he immigrated to the United States, I visited Hyōgo Prefecture, Japan, near the coast of the Japan Sea. During this trip, I discovered that even today Kim has relatives living where his grandfather once did. My visit linked once again the two paths of Kobayashi family history that had diverged from one another when Hideo Kobayashi immigrated to the US.

I also discovered an old family address for Masakuni Okudaira, a settler who became involved in the colony effort after completing his education abroad like Jo Sakai. Okudaira was the second son of Masayuki Okudaira, the last *daimyō*, or regional lord, of Kyushu's Nakatsu Domain. The address led me to greater understanding of this individual and his importance to the colony story.

In general, Japanese society tends to be cool toward individuals who choose to leave family and friends for new lives elsewhere. Leaving the countryside to work in the city, just as immigrating overseas once was, is considered by Japanese to be like abandoning one's origins. People who went abroad, other than those who were famous or who had accomplished some achievement, were apt to be forgotten in Japan.

What this means is that recognition of one's role in American immigration history in a book like *Beikoku Nikkeijin Hyakunen Shi* is a big deal. But to the Japanese American community, a publication such as this contains little to connect the children and grandchildren of the first-generation immigrants to Japanese society as it was known by the first generation. The documentation for such a book unfortunately conveys almost nothing to the Japanese American community, because second- and third-generation Japanese Americans may not understand the Japanese language very well. Possessing documents from the past that they are unable to read, the younger generations cannot pass down the information that they contain.

For this reason, neither the motivations behind the immigrants' decisions to leave home nor their personal stories of living in America have been preserved as a part of history. Instead, this information has been lost. While Japanese American history may exist as a field of study, it is concerned strictly with events that occurred in the United States, with little connection to Japan. The immigrants' stories, however, spanned both countries and their cultures. Between them, the immigrants' emotional attachments swung back and forth constantly, as they did for George Morikami, who often pondered what he should do, whether he should return to Japan or not.

Having uncovered the facts in this way, I decided I wanted to try telling the stories of ordinary people like George Morikami and Jo Sakai, who lived lives that linked two countries and their cultures, and to tell their stories against the background of the times in which they lived. My reason for writing this book and wanting to deal with such themes extends from the fact that, as trivial as it may seem, I too am a Japanese who lived in Florida for a time and wants to leave behind a legacy.

As I write this postscript, I want to express my deeply felt gratitude to all who gave up their time to cooperate in gathering the material for this book.

Whenever I visited, everyone in Florida associated with the Morikami Museum and Japanese Gardens was most helpful, especially James and Chieko Mihori, who generously provided me with details regarding the establishment of Morikami Park as well as their personal reminiscences of George Morikami himself. John Gregersen, cultural director of the Morikami Museum, made recommendations of specific research materials regarding the Yamato Colony and answered my many questions. Thanks to his help I was able to satisfy in my own mind a number of concerns about the colony's history.

From Tamotsu (Tom) Kobayashi, who was raised from infancy at the colony site and who lived there for many years, I heard valuable stories through the cooperation of his son, Kim Kobayashi. Today residing in New Jersey, Sumiko Kobayashi lived in the colony until the age of two. Without the manuscript about the Yamato Colony that she compiled over many years' time, I could not have learned about the kind of life that the colonists led. What is more, a thick diary that Henry Kamiya kept for many years, now in the collection of the Morikami Museum, also proved to be a wonderful historical resource. Written in Japanese with a little English mixed in, the diary focuses on the hardships of running Kamiya's farming enterprise, as well as his relationships with other Yamato settlers, neighbors, and employees.

Research materials and records of the past held in the collections of Virginia Snyder, with whom George Morikami became acquainted late in life, the Boca Raton Historical Society, and the Delray Beach Historical Society proved to be terrific references. I want to thank the staffs of the libraries and local history museums that I visited in the United

States for being so open and accommodating, and for the advice they shared regarding my research.

From an interview with Joe Tashiro and his wife, Yoko, and from photographs of the past in the Tashiro home, I learned a great deal about the early days of Miami Beach development.

Pursuing research in Texas, I met members of the Hirasaki and Sakai families through arrangements made by Gary Nakamura, president of the Houston chapter of the Japanese American Citizens League. The two families are descendants of former Texas pioneers. A tour of a site that was once a Japanese settlement in Texas was a moving experience.

While gathering materials in Japan, I often called on Kazuaki Ida, the grandson of George Morikami's younger sister, at his house in Miyazu. From him I learned about the Morigami family and Takiba, the neighborhood where Morikami played as a child. What is today Ida's house was that where young Sukeji lived before immigrating to the United States. I was also able to meet with Masato Morigami, the grandson of George Morikami's younger brother Masabei. Sharing stories relating to Morikami's time as a young man, Atsuko Kusuda, who also lives locally, provided me with valuable information.

From Morikami's niece Akiko Mihama (formerly Okamoto) I was given access to a substantial number of letters that Morikami sent to the Okamoto family in the 1950s and '60s. In these letters, which the family has carefully preserved through the years, Morikami wrote about matters concerning his hometown. Had the letters not existed, I would not know Morikami's motivations and feelings during this time in his life.

Deciphering for me Morikami's difficult-to-read penmanship was Sadao Yagame, my senior colleague from my days as a newspaper reporter. Reading the letters on my own would have taken up many long hours, so it is no exaggeration to say that this book in its present form owes a great deal to Yagame-*san*'s much-appreciated assistance. Coming close to providing as true an image of the elderly farmer as his letters, Akira Suwa's photographs of Morikami in his later years proved to be a much-valued resource. My thanks to Suwa-*san*, who has been active as a professional photographer in the United States, for readily giving me his permission to use some of his images.

The activities of Jo Sakai, who studied at Dōshisha University, are largely unknown before he immigrated to the United States, but

Suetake Ōmiya suggested different ways of dealing with this lack of information. In addition, I was able to make contact with Hiroshi Mitobe, a grandson of Jo Sakai, as well as Kyō and Takako Sakai, also related to him.

Without the research into the records of departing colonists that Morihiro Oki, grandson of Mitsusaburo Oki, conducted on his own, I would have no understanding of the overall scope of immigration from Miyazu and the Tango Peninsula. About Masakuni Okudaira, his granddaughter Kazue Okudaira revealed to me many details, including the Okudaira family's place in Japanese history.

Regarding Hatsu Odani, George Morikami's first love, I came to know the circumstances concerning their exchange of correspondence through my interview with Hideyo Odani, Hatsu's grandson. From Teruko Yamazaki, Hatsu's niece, I gained an understanding of her life in brief.

In Miyazu and on the Tango Peninsula, Hiroaki Yokotani and Chiemi Nagahama of the Miyazu City Office, no matter how often I sought their help, cheerfully assisted my efforts to gather information about the colonists and their backgrounds. From Tomoko Okamoto of the Miyazu City Library I also received considerable assistance. Kazuhiro Kawamori of the Miyazu Board of Education and Katsuyuki Shintani of the Kyōtango Board of Education gave me their insights from the point of view of local history.

I wanted to know as much as I could about the *chirimen*, or silk crepe, industry since it produced the funding that made the pioneering enterprise in Florida a reality. Conversations with Takamichi and Midori Yoshimura of Yoshimura Shōten, which today continues to produce and market silk crepe, and with *chirimen* scholar Yuko Kitano allowed me to grasp the full picture of the Tango silk crepe industry's involvement. Furthermore, through my introduction to Toshio Shioda, a reporter for the *Mainichi Shimbun* newspaper assigned to Kyōtango City on the Tango Peninsula, I was able to have a productive discussion of this subject.

About the sea route that brought Morikami to the United States and the ship on which he sailed, I appreciated the clear explanation provided by Hakuei Wakiya of the NYK Maritime Museum in Yokohama. On the subject of passports during the period of early immigration from Japan and other similar matters, I received tremendous cooperation from the archives of the Japanese Foreign Ministry. Other archives that helped me to find information about Jo Sakai's personal history were located in the libraries of New York University and Dōshisha University, Kyōto.

Shigeru Kojima of the Japanese Overseas Migration Museum in Yokohama assisted me while I looked into questions regarding Japanese immigration to the United States as a whole. I also received words of advice and encouragement from Masako Iino, president of Tsuda College and a specialist on Japanese immigration to the US. My exchanges with Tatsuya Sudō, Nobuko Awaya, Minoru Kanda, and others of the Ajiakei-Amerikajin Kenkyū Kai (Asian American Study Society) inspired me to continue gathering material for the book. I will never forget such friends who assisted me when I struggled with the final drafts of my manuscript.

Looking back, I see that my relationship with Florida has endured many years. Even today I continue to exchange correspondence with the many friends and acquaintances from the days of my one-year residency in Florida. I would like to thank these friends whom I have known for so long:

> Dr. Roger K. Lewis and his wife, Elizabeth, to whom I am indebted for their gracious hospitality as one of my host families
> Lou and Isilda Lomoriello, another host family
> Bob and Shiiko Alexander, who always greeted me in a cheerful manner
> Robert and Maya Nolin, to whom I am grateful for their generous hospitality whenever I visited Florida in the years since I lived there
> Christopher Nolin, musician and younger brother of Robert, and his wife, Sadako
> Kensuke Ozaki, who has worked in the export-import business in Miami for many years, and his wife, Tomoko

Thanks to friends such as these who always welcomed me warmly, I felt that I could have continued to gather material if necessary, and for that I am deeply grateful.

In addition, I am indebted to those who assisted me in gathering information from many different sources, one fact at a time. Although I am unable to mention all of their names, I would like to thank them most sincerely.

Recently, a certain kind of television show has become popular in Japan. Such programs feature a reporter who travels across the globe seeking places where Japanese are living outside of Japan. In his report from the overseas locale, the astonishment and doubt of the on-screen reporter may be quite apparent: "A Japanese in this kind of place?" he may ask incredulously. "Why is this person living here?"

Perhaps the Japanese of the Yamato Colony were the first to surprise us in this manner. Who were they? Why did they travel to such a place as southern Florida? What did they hope to accomplish? My hope is that readers of this book who have such questions will learn about ordinary people who sought to live where free will and destiny balanced one another.

Florida just happened to be the place where I spent a year in the US twenty-nine years ago, but by the time my year was up, it had come to possess indelible memories for me. At the time, my family cheerfully allowed me the opportunity to have such experiences. To them I apologize for having waited so long to express my gratitude for their understanding and thoughtfulness.

Over the years I have worked on a variety of nonfiction book projects with Hiroyasu Kiuchi, my editor at Junpōsha, publisher of the Japanese edition of this book. Once again I want to express my thanks to Kiuchi-san for guiding me through the publishing process.

Ryusuke Kawai
June 2015

BIBLIOGRAPHY

Japanese-Language Sources

Asao, Naohiro. *Kyōto-fu no Rekishi* (京都府の歴史 History of Kyōto Prefecture). Tōkyō: Yamakawa Shuppansha, 1999.

Beikoku Nikkeijin Hyakunen Shi: Zaibei Nikkeijin Hatten Jinshiroku (米國日系人百年史 在米日系人発展人士録 One Hundred Years of Japanese American History: Individuals Who Contributed to the Growth of the Japanese American Community). Los Angeles: Shin Nichibei Shimbunsha, 1961.

Chōhōsha, ed. *Risshin Chifu: Kaigai Tokō Annai* (立身致富 海外渡航案内 Pull Yourself Up and Seek Your Fortune: A Guide to Going Abroad). Tōkyō: Rakuseisha, 1911.

Foreign Ministry of Japan. *Nihon Gaikō Bunsho* (日本外交文書 Japanese Diplomatic Record) Digital Archives. Vol. 3. 1913. https://www.mofa.go.jp/mofaj/annai/honsho/shiryo/archives/t2-3.html.

Fujioka, Shiro. *Ayumi no Ato: Hokubei Tairiku Nihonjin Kaitaku Monogatari* (歩みの跡 北米大陸日本人開拓物語 Traces of Their Footsteps: The Story of Pioneering Japanese in North America). Los Angeles: Ayumi no Ato Kankō Kōenkai, 1957.

Japanese American Commercial Weekly (*Nichibei Shūhō* 日米週報). 1905–6.

Katayama, Sen. *To-Bei no Hiketsu* (渡米之秘訣 Secrets of Immigrating to America). Tōkyō: To-Bei Kyōkai, n.d.

Kikumura-Yano, Akemi, ed. *Amerika Tairiku Nikkeijin Hyakka Jiten* (アメリカ大陸日系人百科事典 Encyclopedia of Japanese Descendants in the Americas). Translated by Masayo Ohara. Tōkyō: Akashi Shoten, 2002.

Kobayashi, Shigeru. *Mineyama Yawa, Jōkan* (峰山夜話 上巻 Evening Chats in Mineyama, Volume One). Mineyama, Japan: Tango Kinrōsha Bunka Dantai Renmei, 1973.

Mamiya, Kunio. *Saibara Seitō Kenkyū* (西原清東研究 The Study of Seitō Saibara). Kochi, Japan: Kochi Municipal Library, n.d.

Miyazu City History Editorial Board. *Miyazu-shi Shi: Tsūshi Hen Gekan* (宮津市史 通史編下巻 History of Miyazu City: Economic History, Volume Two). Miyazu, Japan: Miyazu City Office, 2004.

Murayama, Yūzō. *Amerika ni Ikita Nihonjin Imin Nikkei Issei no Hikari to Kage* (アメリカに生きた日本人移民日系一世の光と影 Immigration of Japanese Living in the United States: The First Generation of Japanese Americans in Darkness and in Light). Tōkyō: Tōyō Keizai Shimbunsha, 1989.

Naka-Gun Ippan Mineyama Annai (中郡一斑 峰山案内 Guide to Mineyama, a Part of Naka County). Mineyama, Japan: Yodotoku Shoten, 1911.

Nomura, Tatsurō. *Tairiku Kokka Amerika no Tenkai* (大陸国家アメリカの展開 The Development of America, Continent and Nation). Tōkyō: Yamakawa Shuppansha, 1996.

Okabe, Makio. *Umi o Watatta Nihonjin* (海を渡った日本人 The Japanese Who Crossed the Sea). Tōkyō: Yamakawa Shuppansha, 2002.

Sadō, Takuhei. *Kariforunia Imin Monogatari* (カリフォルニア移民物語 The Story of California Immigration). Tōkyō: Aki Shobo, 1998.

Shiryō Tenkyō Gijuku Gekan (資料天橋義塾下巻 Documentary Materials for the Tenkyō Academy, Volume Two). Miyazu, Japan: Miyazu-shi Kyōiku Iinkai, et al., 1979.

Tamura, Norio, and Shiramizu Shigehiko, eds. *Beikoku Shoki no Nihongo Shimbun* (米国初期の日本語新聞 Early Japanese-Language Newspapers in the United States). Tōkyō: Keisō Shobo, 1986.

Tokubetsu-Ten Zuroku: Tango Chirimen (特別展図録 丹後縮緬 Tango Silk Crepe: Catalogue to the Special Exhibition). Miyazu, Japan: Kyōto Furitsu Tango Kyōdo Shiryōkan, 1989.

Tsuruya, Hisashi. *Amerika Seibu Kaitaku to Nihonjin* (アメリカ西部開拓と日本人 Japanese and the Opening of the American West). Tōkyō: NHK Books, 1977.

Tsutsui, Tadashi. *Ikkaku Senkin no Yume: Hokubei Imin no Ayumi* (一攫千金の夢 北米移民の歩み The Dream of Getting Rich Quickly: Steps to North American Immigration). Tsu, Japan: Mie Daigaku Shuppankai, 2003.

———. *Shinsho Amerika Gasshūkoku Shi 2: Furonteia to Matenrō* (新書アメリカ合衆国史2 フロンティアと摩天楼 The Shinsho History of the United States, Volume Two: Frontier and Skyscrapers). Tōkyō: Kōdansha Gendai Shinsho, 1989.

Walls, Thomas K. *Tekisasu no Nikkeijin* (テキサスの日系人 The Japanese Texans). Translated by Kunio Mamiya. Tōkyō: Fuyō Shobo Shuppan, 1997.

Yagishita, Hiroko. "Senzenki no Ryōken no Hensen (戦前期の旅券の変遷 Changes in Passports During the Pre-War Period)." *Gaikō Shiryōkan Hō* (Bulletin of the Diplomatic Archives) No. 12 (June 1998): 31–59.

Yamane, Goichi. *Saikin To-Bei Annai* (最近渡米案内 Most Recent Information on Immigration to the United States). Tōkyō: To-Bei Zasshi-sha, 1906.

Yokohama to Kinu no Hyakunen (横浜と絹の百年 One Hundred Years of Yokohama and Silk). Yokohama: Yokohama Raw Silk Exchange, 1994.

English-Language Sources

Aronson, Virginia. *Konnichiwa Florida Moon: The Story of George Morikami.* Sarasota, FL: Pineapple Press, 2002.

Curl, Donald W., ed. "Yamato." *Spanish River Papers* 6, no. 1 (October 1977).

———. "T. M. Rickards and the Founding of the Japanese Colony." *Spanish River Papers* 3, no. 2 (February 1980).

"Eighty Years Ago . . . Defection from the Japanese Colony and Settlement at Last." *Morikami Quarterly.* August 1985.

"Eighty Years Ago . . . The Future of the Japanese Colony in Jeopardy." *Morikami Newsletter.* July 1984.

"Eighty Years Ago . . . The Story of the Japanese Colony Called Yamato Begins . . ." *Morikami Newsletter.* December 1983.

Gitlow, Abraham L. *New York University's Stern School of Business: A Centennial Retrospective.* New York: NYU Press, 1995.

Kobayashi, Sumiko. "Yamato, Florida: A Japanese Farming Village Between Palm Beach and the Everglades." Unpublished manuscript, April 2008. Copy in the Morikami Museum archives.

Ling, Sally J. *A History of Boca Raton.* Charleston, SC: History Press, 2007.

Lloyd, Joanne M. "Yankees of the Orient: Yamato and Japanese Immigration to America." MA thesis, Florida Atlantic University, 1990.

Lynfield, Geoffrey. "Yamato and Morikami: The Story of the Japanese Colony and Some of its Settlers." *Spanish River Papers* 13, no. 3 (Spring 1985).

Martin, Sidney Walter. *Henry Flagler: Visionary of the Gilded Age.* Lake Buena Vista, FL: Tailored Tours Publications, 1998.

Morikami Museum staff. *The Yamato Colony: Japanese Pioneers in Florida.* Delray Beach, FL: Morikami Museum and Japanese Gardens, 2009.

Pozzetta, George E. "Foreign Colonies in South Florida, 1865–1910." *Tequesta: The Journal of The Historical Association of Southern Florida* No. 34 (1974): 45–54.

Pozzetta, George E., and Harry A. Kersey Jr. "Yamato Colony: A Japanese Presence in South Florida." *Tequesta: The Journal of The Historical Association of Southern Florida* No. 36 (1976): 66–77.

Russell, Jesse, and Ronald Cohn, eds. *Yamato Colony, Florida.* Edinburgh, Scotland: Lennex Corporation, 2012.

Snyder, Virginia. "Soul Survivor." *Palm Beach Life,* May 1993.

Soto, Ana M. "The Yamato Colony during World War II." *Tustenegee* 3, no. 2 (October 2012). http://www.pbchistoryonline.org/uploads/file/Yamato%20Colony. pdf.

Standiford, Les. *Last Train to Paradise.* New York: Broadway Paperbacks, 2002.

Spanish River Papers 1, no. 2 (May 1973).

Transcript, oral history interview of George Morikami conducted by George E. Pozzetta with Dr. Harry A. Kersey, June 11, 1974. Samuel Proctor Oral History Program Collection, P. K. Yonge Library of Florida History, University of Florida. http://ufdc.ufl.edu/UF00006626/00001/1j?search=george+%3dmorikami.

"Women in Boca Raton: Fifty Years of History." *Spanish River Papers* 17 (August 1993).

In addition to these resources, I consulted materials in the collection of the Morikami Museum and the Virginia Snyder Collection at the S. E. Wimberly Library, Florida Atlantic University. I also viewed newspaper articles published in Florida between 1903 and the present reporting on the Yamato Colony and the activities of George Morikami and other colonists.

INDEX

112, 116–19, 132, 164–65, 167, 177, 181;
Road, ix–x, 154; Rock, 123, 167; Vil-
lage, 58, 70
Yoshida, Gengoro, 76, 110

Ryusuke Kawai began his journalism career with the *Mainichi Shimbun* newspaper in 1980 after earning a B.A. degree in political science from Keio University. In 1986, he left Japan for an internship with the *Daytona Beach News-Journal* in Florida. A member of the Japan Writers' Association, Mr. Kawai currently works in a freelance capacity. In 2016 he published a Japanese-language translation of John Okada's novel, *No-No Boy,* a milestone in Japanese American literature.

John Gregersen earned an M.A. degree in Japanese studies from the University of Michigan in 1977. He joined the staff of the Morikami Museum and Japanese Gardens in 1978 as assistant curator, rising to senior curator and cultural director over a thirty-five-year career with the museum. In 2013, Mr. Gregersen received the Foreign Minister's Commendation awarded by the Japanese Foreign Ministry and the Consulate-General of Japan in Miami.

A native of Japan, Reiko Nishioka earned an M.A. degree in museum leadership from the Bank Street College of Education, New York City, in 1990. She served as director of education at the Morikami Museum and Japanese Gardens for a period of twenty years beginning in 1992. Ms. Nishioka was a recipient of the Foreign Minister's Commendation in 2015.